Walt Whitman

Edited with annotations and introduction by
ELLMAN CRASNOW
University of East Anglia

WEIDENFELD & NICOLSON

First published in 1996 by J M Dent
This edition published in 2023 by Weidenfeld & Nicolson
An imprint of The Orion Publishing Group Ltd
Carmelite House
50 Victoria Embankment
London
EC4Y 0DZ

An Hachette UK Company

1 3 5 7 9 10 8 6 4 2

A CIP catalogue record for this book is available from the British Library.

ISBN mmp: 978 1 3996 1413 9
ISBN ebook: 978 1 3996 1414 6

Printed in the UK by Clays Ltd, Elcograf S.p.A.

www.orionbooks.co.uk
www.weidenfeldandnicolson.co.uk

Contents

Note on the Author and Editor

WALT WHITMAN was born on Long Island in 1819; his struggling family came from English, Dutch and Welsh stock. His early occupations in Brooklyn, Long Island and Manhattan included journalism, printing and school teaching, and he was active in Democratic Party politics. He thrived on reading and reviewing, museum and library visits, lectures, theatre and opera, and the vivid life of the city streets, mixing with both workers and bohemians, and appearing at different times as a dandy or as a 'rough'.

Whitman had written sentimental poems and stories, and a temperance novel, before finding his own voice in the fifties. The first edition of *Leaves of Grass* (1855) was praised by Emerson; and Whitman, ever active in self-promotion, printed Emerson's words in his second edition, in which he also bewailed the lack of an 'unabashed development of sex'. His attempts to remedy this lack, notably in the 1860 edition, caused the loss of a government job in 1865, and a threatened prosecution in 1882, but he never wavered in his purpose.

Visiting his wounded brother George during the Civil War in 1862, Whitman began to tend the soldiers, and in Washington he took up a taxing round of hospital visits. He remained in Washington after the war and formed his closest relationship, with a young street-car conductor called Peter Doyle, but a stroke later forced him to live with George in Camden, New Jersey. He recovered sufficiently to take a Western trip in 1879; recognition gradually increased, and he was able to buy his own house in Camden. After publishing his final, so-called 'Death-bed Edition', he died in 1892.

ELLMAN CRASNOW worked as an architect before turning to literature and studying at Cambridge and Yale; he now lectures on English and American Literature at the University of East Anglia. He has published on aspects of American writing from the colonial period to the present day, on modern poetry and on literary theory.

Chronology of Whitman's Life

Year	Age	Life
1819		Born 31 May, on Long Island; second child of Walter Whitman, house builder, and Louisa Van Velsor
1823	3	Whitman family moves to Brooklyn
1825–30	6–11	Whitman attends public school in Brooklyn
1831–5	12–16	Learns printing trade; various jobs as printer and compositor
1833	14	Family moves back to Long Island, but Whitman stays in Brooklyn
1836–8	16–19	School teaching, subsequently resumed at intervals. Membership of debating societies
1838–9	19–20	Publishes and edits the weekly *Long-Islander*; writes poetry and prose
1840	21	Works for Martin Van Buren's presidential campaign
1841	22	Moves to New York City; printing work, Democratic party politics. Publishes stories
1842–7	23–8	Various jobs as journalist and editor. Publishes stories, and *Franklin Evans* (1842), a temperance novel. Follows theatre and opera in New York

Chronology of his Times

Year	Literary Context	Historical Events
1819		Purchase of Florida from Spain
1823		Proclamation of the Monroe Doctrine
1829		Andrew Jackson elected President of the US
1831		William Lloyd Garrison founds the abolitionist *Liberator*
1834		Cyrus McCormick's grain reaper patented
1836	Ralph Waldo Emerson, *Nature*; Thomas Carlyle, *Sartor Resartus*	
1837		First military use of Colt weapons in the Seminole war
1839	Edgar Allan Poe, *Tales of the Grotesque and Arabesque*	
1840		US population reaches 17 million
1841	Emerson, *Essays* (first series)	
1842	Alfred Tennyson, *Poems*	
1844	Emerson, *Essays* (second series)	

Year	Age	Life
1848	29	Three months in New Orleans as editor of the *Crescent*
1848–9	29–30	Edits *Brooklyn Freeman*
1850–4	31–5	Freelance journalism, topical poems. House building. Runs printing office and stationery store
1855	36	First (anonymous) edition of *Leaves of Grass*. Father dies
1856	37	Second edition of *Leaves of Grass*, with author's name; includes congratulatory letter from Ralph Waldo Emerson, with Whitman's reply, and a selection of reviews
1857–9	37–40	Edits *Brooklyn Times*
1860	40	Third edition of *Leaves of Grass*, published in Boston

Year	Literary Context	Historical Events
1845		Texas annexed
1846–8		US–Mexico war; New Mexico and California ceded to US
1849		California Gold Rush Fugitive Slave Law
1850	Nathaniel Hawthorne, *The Scarlet Letter*; Tennyson, *In Memoriam*; William Wordsworth, *The Prelude* (published posthumously)	
1851	Herman Melville, *Moby-Dick*	
1852	Harriet Beecher Stowe, *Uncle Tom's Cabin*	
1854	Henry David Thoreau, *Walden*	Republican Party re-formed on an anti-slavery basis Commodore Perry's fleet visits Japan
1855	Henry Wadsworth Longfellow, *The Song of Hiawatha*; Robert Browning, *Men and Women*	
1858		Abraham Lincoln enters Senate as a Republican
1859		John Brown's raid on Harper's Ferry
1860		Nation linked by Morse's telegraph system Lincoln elected President
1861	Charles Dickens, *Great Expectations*	American Civil War begins

Year	Age	Life
1862–4	43–4	Visits brother George, wounded at Fredericksburg; remains in Washington DC, visiting soldiers in hospital. Part-time work in Army Paymaster's office
1865	45	Clerk in Department of Interior, and Attorney General's office. *Drum-Taps* and *Sequel to Drum-Taps*
1867	48	Fourth edition of *Leaves of Grass*
1868	49	William Rossetti's expurgated selection, *Poems of Walt Whitman*, published in England
1871	50–51	Fifth edition of *Leaves of Grass*. *Democratic Vistas*. Receives poem from Swinburne, letter from Tennyson
1873	53–4	Paralytic stroke. Mother dies. Goes to live with brother George in Camden, New Jersey
1875	56	'Centennial Edition' of *Leaves of Grass* (dated 1876)
1879	60	First trip to the West
1881	62	Seventh edition of *Leaves of Grass*, final arrangement of most of the poems
1882	62–3	Meeting with Oscar Wilde. *Specimen Days and Collect*, including Whitman's account of his Civil War experiences. Threatened prosecution of *Leaves of Grass* for obscenity; the resultant publicity boosts sales and royalties
1884	65	Whitman now able to buy his own house in Camden

Year	Literary Context	Historical Events
1863		Lincoln's Emancipation Proclamation
1865		Civil War ends
		Lincoln assassinated
1866		Formation of the Ku Klux Klan
1867		Alaska purchased from Russia
1868–9	Browning, *The Ring and the Book*	
1869		First transcontinental railroad completed
1870		Standard Oil Company formed
1871–4	George Eliot, *Middlemarch*	
1876		Alexander Graham Bell invents the telephone
1877		First nationwide strike in US history
1881	Henry James, *The Portrait of a Lady*	
1884	Mark Twain, *Adventures of Huckleberry Finn*	

Year	Age	Life
1888	69	Another paralytic stroke, and severe illness. *November Boughs*
1889	70	Eighth edition of *Leaves of Grass*
1890	71	John Addington Symonds offers homosexual interpretation of the 'Calamus' poems, indignantly rejected by Whitman: 'I have had six children'
1891	72	'Authorized' or 'Deathbed' edition of *Leaves of Grass* (dated 1891–2)
1892	72	Whitman dies on 26 March. *Complete Prose Works*

Year	Literary Context	Historical Events
1885	William Dean Howells, *The Rise of Silas Lapham*	
1886	Death of Emily Dickinson	Anarchist riot in Haymarket Square, Chicago Foundation of the American Federation of Labor
1888	Edward Bellamy, *Looking Backward*	
1891	William James, *The Principles of Psychology*	

Introduction

Poetry is often seen as an elitist art: written by the few, read by the few. What happens, then, when a truly democratic poet begins to write in nineteenth-century America, full of patriotic enthusiasm for his new society? Whitman was such a poet, and his mission was not simple. On the one hand, he wanted to bring his fellow-citizens all the insights that a great national poet could offer; but on the other hand, he did not want to separate himself from them by seeming superior in any way. His strategies for solving this problem lie at the heart of his poetry.

We can begin by looking at Whitman's attitude to the Muse. The Muses were sister goddesses in ancient Greece who inspired the various arts, and European poets had for centuries invoked the aid of the Muse of poetry in producing their works. This image of ancient culture aroused some suspicion in nineteenth-century America; already in 1837 Ralph Waldo Emerson, the great thinker of his day, had warned his compatriots 'We have listened too long to the courtly Muses of Europe'. Whitman heeded this warning; but late in his career he did imagine inviting the Muse to migrate from Europe and leave the ancient epics behind; he pictured her entering the American scene:

> Making directly for this rendezvous, vigorously clearing a path for
> herself, striding through the confusion,
> By thud of machinery and shrill steam-whistle undismay'd,
> Bluff'd not a bit by drain-pipe, gasometers, artificial fertilizers,
> Smiling and pleas'd with palpable intent to stay,
> She's here, install'd amid the kitchen ware![1]

This comic setting of steam-whistle and gasometers has its serious side. American poetry, as Whitman saw it, could not afford to dwell on the heights; it had to come down to the city streets, to the gritty realities of common life, if it was to exist at all.

In fact, the Muse is not really needed by the self-reliant voice that says 'I' in Whitman's poetry. This 'I' is not simply to be identified with the author, for in poems such as 'Song of Myself' it is somehow both an individual and a composite figure that can encompass the whole nation:

> I celebrate myself, and sing myself,
> And what I shall assume you shall assume,
> For every atom belonging to me as good belongs to you.

The tensions of a democratic poetry are already clear in this extract. At first the speaker celebrates himself and seems to be a sage – 'what I assume you shall assume'. But then he draws back, for he does not want to seem superior to his audience; after all, what is his is also theirs. As 'A Song for Occupations' has it, 'I bring you what you much need yet already have'. The democratic audience should already possess the qualities that it needs; it must simply be reminded of its own potential:

> Will you rot your own fruit in yourself there?
> Will you squat and stifle there?[2]

It is in one sense the audience itself that speaks, while the 'I' merely enables it to speak:

> (It is you talking just as much as myself, I act as the tongue of you,
> Tied in your mouth, in mine it begins to be loosen'd.)[3]

In this mood, Whitman's speaker is self-effacing, for he is merely a means of expression, 'the tongue of you', rather than a superior poet; he accordingly avoids traditional poetic procedures. But when the speaker becomes a composite figure of his society, self-esteem replaces self-effacement: 'I celebrate myself'. It looks almost like a contradiction, but then contradictions are part of Whitman's plan, since they affirm the inclusiveness of his composite figure:

> Do I contradict myself?
> Very well then I contradict myself,
> (I am large, I contain multitudes.)[4]

This inclusiveness in Whitman's poetry is typically expressed by a list or catalogue; section 15 of 'Song of Myself' is a good example. Here society's various individuals coexist – each, usually, has a single line – side by side in a state of democratic equality. There is no sense that one is ranked above another, and the speaker seems to emerge out of them:

> And these tend inward to me, and I tend outward to them,
> And such as it is to be of these more or less I am,
> And of these one and all I weave the song of myself.

All this talk of an inclusive voice or a composite figure can sound very abstract, and this abstraction is a danger for the poet's imagined relationship with his audience. It may make that relationship seem to be nothing more than an idea or a figure of speech. Of course, Whitman wants to avoid giving that impression; in order to strengthen the relationship, he makes his 'I' identify itself, not just with the community, but with vividly individual experience:

> Not a cholera patient lies at the last gasp but I also lie at the last gasp,
> My face is ash-color'd, my sinews gnarl, away from me people retreat.[5]

The speaker doesn't just represent different individuals, he claims to *become* them, even in their worst moments: 'I am the man, I suffer'd, I was there'. And this makes the link between the speaker and society's individuals seem actual, concrete rather than abstract.

To emphasize the concrete rather than the abstract is a common strategy in Whitman's writing; it occurs, crucially, in his view of language:

> Language, be it remember'd, is not an abstract construction of the learn'd, or of dictionary-makers, but is something arising out of the work, needs, ties, joys, affections, tastes, of long generations of humanity, and has its bases broad and low, close to the ground. Its final decisions are made by the masses, people nearest the concrete, having most to do with actual land and sea.[6]

Language is seen as a concrete and communal activity; and the word itself is not an abstract symbol, but rather humanized by association with the body:

> Human bodies are words, myriads of words,
> (In the best poems re-appears the body, man's or woman's, well-shaped, natural, gay . . .[7]

This concentration on the body, in turn, produces the characteristic sensuality and sexuality of Whitman's poetry. Sexuality is welcomed for itself, and also because it shows the way in which, ideally, people should interact: honestly, intimately, affectionately. In a group of poems published in 1860, the 'adhesiveness' of male homoeroticism becomes an emblem of the way in which society should cohere:

> I will make inseparable cities with their arms about each other's
>   necks,
>   By the love of comrades,
>   By the manly love of comrades.[8]

Whitman is not only a homoerotic poet; indeed, he is generally and genuinely liberating in his attacks on repressive propriety for both men and women. But his venture 'In Paths Untrodden' (as one title puts it) has a special intensity in its move against the ostracism of homoerotic desire. Of all the excluded and marginalized figures that are reabsorbed into his body politic, these covert lovers are perhaps most eagerly welcomed:

> I will play a part no longer, why should I exile myself from my
>   companions?
> O you shunn'd persons, I at least do not shun you,
> I come forthwith in your midst, I will be your poet,
> I will be more to you than to any of the rest.[9]

To celebrate the erotic body is often to idealize it, and there are many chants of 'types of athletic love' or 'the exquisite realization of health' in Whitman's work. But if this were all, if only the well-shaped body were to be presented, then democratic inclusiveness would dwindle into a mere cult. We have already seen, through the example of the cholera patient, that this is not allowed to happen. It was an historic event that produced Whitman's great encounter with the flawed and broken body – the inferno of the American Civil War:

> Faces, varieties, postures beyond description, most in obscurity, some of
>   them dead,
> Surgeons operating, attendants holding lights, the smell of ether, the
>   odor of blood,
> The crowd, O the crowd of the bloody forms . . .[10]

His extraordinary combination of pity, horror and eroticism can be seen in poems like 'The Wound-Dresser'. Tragedy, however, belongs to all life, and not just to war. To realize the world of pain, loss and death is thus seen as a necessary initiation for the poet in 'Out of the Cradle Endlessly Rocking'. Even Whitman's 'I', his grand composite figure, is not invulnerable. In 'As I Ebb'd with the Ocean

of Life' it becomes a drowned corpse, just one of the floating
fragments of sea-wrack:

> Me and mine, loose windrows, little corpses,
> Froth, snowy white, and bubbles,
> (See, from my dead lips the ooze exuding at last,
> See, the prismatic colors glistening and rolling,)
> Tufts of straw, sands, fragments . . .

Whitman's love of the concrete, the actual and the embodied
drew him away from awkward speculation: 'I accept Reality and
dare not question it'. But he lived in a culture where the
questioning of appearance and reality was pursued by many
writers. His great contemporaries Emerson and Poe, Hawthorne
and Melville, all in their different ways asked metaphysical
questions, questions that went beyond the physical world of
appearances, perhaps to invoke a hidden or spiritual realm.
Whitman too had his spiritual aspirations, but he did not want to
disparage the physical world in which his social and sexual
loyalties lay. Even when he acknowledged that the world of
appearances might indeed be only a show, he accepted this show,
this 'necessary film'. Captain Ahab, in Melville's *Moby-Dick*, rebels
against appearances; he wants to 'strike through the mask'. The
speaker of 'Crossing Brooklyn Ferry', by contrast, welcomes the
appearances that surround him; they may mask mysteries, but
they are friends, not deceptive enemies:

> We use you, and do not cast you aside – we plant you permanently
>   within us,
> We fathom you not – we love you – there is perfection in you also,
> You furnish your parts towards eternity,
> Great or small, you furnish your parts towards the soul.

'We fathom you not': despite its ideal inclusiveness, Whitman's
poetry is also drawn towards what evades it, towards what is
perhaps unknowable and unsayable:

> There is something that comes to one now and perpetually,
> It is not what is printed, preach'd, discussed, it eludes discussion and
>   print,
> It is not to be put in a book, it is not in this book . . .[11]

What 'eludes discussion' becomes an increasingly important theme
in the later poems, with their interest in what lies beyond both word

and world, and in death as a necessary entrance to this realm; these poems 'launch out on trackless seas'. Thus 'A Noiseless Patient Spider' moves far from the jostle of the city streets into 'measureless oceans of space'. Even 'Sparkles from the Wheel', which does present a city group, describes it as if lost in space, 'an unminded point set in a vast surrounding'; its speaker becomes 'a phantom curiously floating'. 'A Clear Midnight' sums up this theme, and a note on its manuscript suggests that Whitman thought it a suitable close for his poetry as a whole. In this valedictory poem, his vast output, the 'endless unfolding of words', at last gives way to a 'free flight into the wordless'. This does not sound like an ending; it reads more like a launch or a release – but it is a release 'into the wordless', into a final realm of experience that must leave physical life and language behind.

ELLMAN CRASNOW

References

1. 'Song of the Exposition', ll.54–58.
2. 'A Song of the Rolling Earth', ll.29–30
3. 'Song of Myself', ll.1248–9
4. ibid, ll.1324–6
5. ibid, ll.955–6
6. 'Slang in America', from *November Boughs*, reprinted in Walt Whitman, *Leaves of Grass* (London: Everyman Paperbacks, 1994) p.561
7. 'A Song of the Rolling Earth', ll.7–8
8. 'For You O Democracy', ll.7–9
9. 'Native Moments', ll.9–12
10. 'A March in the Ranks Hard-Prest, and the Road Unknown', ll.14–16
11. 'A Song for Occupations', ll.44–46

Walt Whitman

There was a Child Went Forth

There was a child went forth every day,
And the first object he look'd upon, that object he became,
And that object became part of him for the day or a certain
    part of the day,
Or for many years or stretching cycles of years.

The early lilacs became part of this child,
And grass and white and red morning-glories, and white and
    red clover, and the song of the phoebe-bird,
And the Third-month lambs and the sow's pink-faint litter,
    and the mare's foal and the cow's calf,
And the noisy brood of the barnyard or by the mire of the
    pond-side,
And the fish suspending themselves so curiously below there,
    and the beautiful curious liquid,
And the water-plants with their graceful flat heads, all
    became part of him.   10

The field-sprouts of Fourth-month and Fifth-month became
    part of him,
Winter-grain sprouts and those of the light-yellow corn, and
    the esculent roots of the garden,
And the apple-trees cover'd with blossoms and the fruit
    afterward, and wood-berries, and the commonest weeds
    by the road,
And the old drunkard staggering home from the outhouse of
    the tavern whence he had lately risen,
And the schoolmistress that pass'd on her way to the school,
And the friendly boys that pass'd, and the quarrelsome boys,
And the tidy and fresh-cheek'd girls, and the barefoot negro
    boy and girl,
And all the changes of city and country wherever he went.

His own parents, he that had father'd him, and she that had
    conceiv'd him in her womb and birth'd him,

They gave this child more of themselves than that,   20
They gave him afterward every day, they became part of him.

The mother at home quietly placing the dishes on the supper-
    table,
The mother with mild words, clean her cap and gown, a
    wholesome odor falling off her person and clothes as she
    walks by,
The father, strong, self-sufficient, manly, mean, anger'd,
    unjust,
The blow, the quick loud word, the tight bargain, the crafty
    lure,
The family usages, the language, the company, the furniture,
    the yearning and swelling heart,
Affection that will not be gainsay'd, the sense of what is real,
    the thought if after all it should prove unreal,
The doubts of day-time and the doubts of night-time, the
    curious whether and how,
Whether that which appears so is so, or is it all flashes and
    specks?
Men and women crowding fast in the streets, if they are not
    flashes and specks what are they?   30
The streets themselves and the façades of houses, and goods
    in the windows,
Vehicles, teams, the heavy-plank'd wharves, the huge cross-
    ing at the ferries,
The village on the highland seen from afar at sunset, the river
    between,
Shadows, aureola and mist, the light falling on roofs and
    gables of white or brown two miles off,
The schooner near by sleepily dropping down the tide, the
    little boat slack-tow'd astern,
The hurrying tumbling waves, quick-broken crests, slapping,
The strata of color'd clouds, the long bar of maroon-tint away
    solitary by itself, the spread of purity it lies motionless in,
The horizon's edge, the flying sea-crow, the fragrance of salt
    marsh and shore mud,
These became part of that child who went forth every day,
    and who now goes, and will always go forth every day.

1855   1871

from **Song of Myself**

1

I celebrate myself, and sing myself,
And what I assume you shall assume,
For every atom belonging to me as good belongs to you.

I loafe and invite my soul,
I lean and loafe at my ease observing a spear of summer grass.

My tongue, every atom of my blood, form'd from this soil,
    this air,
Born here of parents born here from parents the same, and
    their parents the same,
I, now thirty-seven years old in perfect health begin,
Hoping to cease not till death.
Creeds and schools in abeyance,   10
Retiring back a while sufficed at what they are, but never
    forgotten,
I harbor for good or bad, I permit to speak at every hazard,
Nature without check with original energy.

2

Houses and rooms are full of perfumes, the shelves are
    crowded with perfumes,
I breathe the fragrance myself and know it and like it,
The distillation would intoxicate me also, but I shall not let it.

The atmosphere is not a perfume, it has no taste of the
    distillation, it is odorless,
It is for my mouth forever, I am in love with it,
I will go to the bank by the wood and become undisguised and
    naked,
I am mad for it to be in contact with me.   20
The smoke of my own breath,
Echoes, ripples, buzz'd whispers, love-root, silk-thread, crotch
    and vine,

My respiration and inspiration, the beating of my heart, the
    passing of blood and air through my lungs,
The sniff of green leaves and dry leaves, and of the shore and
    dark-color'd sea-rocks, and of hay in the barn,
The sound of the belch'd words of my voice loos'd to the
    eddies of the wind,
A few light kisses, a few embraces, a reaching around of arms,
The play of shine and shade on the trees as the supple boughs
    wag,
The delight alone or in the rush of the streets, or along the
    fields and hill-sides,
The feeling of health, the full-noon trill, the song of me rising
    from bed and meeting the sun.

Have you reckon'd a thousand acres much? have you
    reckon'd the earth much?   30
Have you practis'd so long to learn to read?
Have you felt so proud to get at the meaning of poems?

Stop this day and night with me and you shall possess the
    origin of all poems,
You shall possess the good of the earth and sun, (there are
    millions of suns left,)
You shall no longer take things at second or third hand, nor
    look through the eyes of the dead, nor feed on the specters
    in books,
You shall not look through my eyes either, nor take things
    from me,
You shall listen to all sides and filter them from your self.

3

I have heard what the talkers were talking, the talk of the
    beginning and the end,
But I do not talk of the beginning or the end.

There was never any more inception than there is now,   40
Nor any more youth or age than there is now,
And will never be any more perfection than there is now,
Nor any more heaven or hell than there is now.

*

Urge and urge and urge,
Always the procreant urge of the world.
Out of the dimness opposite equals advance, always sub-
    stance and increase, always sex,
Always a knit of identity, always distinction, always a breed
    of life.

To elaborate is no avail, learn'd and unlearn'd feel that it is so.

Sure as the most certain sure, plumb in the uprights, well
    entretied, braced in the beams,
Stout as a horse, affectionate, haughty, electrical,   50
I and this mystery here we stand.

Clear and sweet is my soul, and clear and sweet is all that is
    not my soul.

Lack one lacks both, and the unseen is proved by the seen,
Till that becomes unseen and receives proof in its turn.

Showing the best and dividing it from the worst age vexes
    age,
Knowing the perfect fitness and equanimity of things, while
    they discuss I am silent, and go bathe and admire myself.
Welcome is every organ and attribute of me, and of any man
    hearty and clean,
Not an inch nor a particle of an inch is vile, and none shall be
    less familiar than the rest.

I am satisfied – I see, dance, laugh, sing;
As the hugging and loving bed-fellow sleeps at my side
    through the night, and withdraws at the peep of the day
    with stealthy tread,   60
Leaving me baskets cover'd with white towels swelling the
    house with their plenty,
Shall I postpone my acceptation and realization and scream
    at my eyes,
That they turn from gazing after and down the road,
And forthwith cipher and show me to a cent,

Exactly the value of one and exactly the value of two, and
    which is ahead?

4

Trippers and askers surround me,
People I meet, the effect upon me of my early life or the ward
    and city I live in, or the nation,
The latest dates, discoveries, inventions, societies, authors old
    and new,
My dinner, dress, associates, looks, compliments, dues,
The real or fancied indifference of some man or woman I love,   70
The sickness of one of my folks or of myself, or ill-doing or loss
    or lack of money, or depressions or exaltations,
Battles, the horrors of fratricidal war, the fever of doubtful
    news, the fitful events;
These come to me days and nights and go from me again,
But they are not the Me myself.

Apart from the pulling and hauling stands what I am,
Stands amused, complacent, compassionating, idle, unitary,
Looks down, is erect, or bends an arm on an impalpable
    certain rest,
Looking with side-curved head curious what will come next,
Both in and out of the game and watching and wondering at
    it.

Backward I see in my own days where I sweated through fog
    with linguists and contenders,   80
I have no mockings or arguments, I witness and wait.

5

I believe in you my soul, the other I am must not abase itself to
    you,
And you must not be abased to the other,

Loafe with me on the grass, loose the stop from your throat,
Not words, not music or rhyme I want, not custom or lecture,
    not even the best,
Only the lull I like, the hum of your valvèd voice.

I mind how once we lay such a transparent summer
    morning,
How you settled your head athwart my hips and gently
    turn'd over upon me,
And parted the shirt from my bosom-bone, and plunged your
    tongue to my bare-stript heart,
And reach'd till you felt my beard, and reach'd till you held
    my feet.   90

Swiftly arose and spread around me the peace and knowledge
    that pass all the argument of the earth,
And I know that the hand of God is the promise of my own,
And I know that the spirit of God is the brother of my own,
And that all the men ever born are also my brothers, and the
    women my sisters and lovers,
And that a kelson of the creation is love,
And limitless are leaves stiff or drooping in the fields,
And brown ants in the little wells beneath them,
And mossy scabs of the worm fence, heap'd stones, elder,
    mullein and poke-weed.

6
A child said *What is the grass?* fetching it to me with full
    hands;
How could I answer the child? I do not know what it is any
    more than he.   100

I guess it must be the flag of my disposition, out of hopeful
    green stuff woven.
Or I guess it is the handkerchief of the Lord,
A scented gift and remembrancer designedly dropt,
Bearing the owner's name someway in the corners, that we
    may see and remark, and say *Whose?*

Or I guess the grass is itself a child, the produced babe of the
    vegetation.

Or I guess it is a uniform hieroglyphic,
And it means, Sprouting alike in broad zones and narrow
    zones,

Growing among black folks as among white,
Kanuck, Tuckahoe, Congressman, Cuff, I give them the same,
    I receive them the same.

And now it seems to me the beautiful uncut hair of graves.   110

Tenderly will I use you curling grass,
It may be you transpire from the breasts of young men,
It may be if I had known them I would have loved them,
It may be you are from old people, or from offspring taken
    soon out of their mothers' laps,
And here you are the mothers' laps.

This grass is very dark to be from the white heads of old
    mothers,
Darker than the colorless beards of old men,
Dark to come from under the faint red roofs of mouths.

O I perceive after all so many uttering tongues,
And I perceive they do not come from the roofs of mouths for
    nothing.   120

I wish I could translate the hints about the dead young men
    and women,
And the hints about old men and mothers, and the offspring
    taken soon out of their laps.

What do you think has become of the young and old men?
And what do you think has become of the women and
    children?

They are alive and well somewhere,
The smallest sprout shows there is really no death,
And if ever there was it led forward life, and does not wait at
    the end to arrest it,
And ceas'd the moment life appear'd.

All goes onward and outward, nothing collapses,
And to die is different from what any one supposed, and
    luckier.   130

7

Has any one supposed it lucky to be born?
I hasten to inform him or her it is just as lucky to die, and I
    know it.

I pass death with the dying and birth with the new-wash'd
    babe, and am not contain'd between my hat and boots,
And peruse manifold objects, no two alike and every one
    good,
The earth good and the stars good, and their adjuncts all
    good.

I am not an earth nor an adjunct of an earth,
I am the mate and companion of people, all just as immortal
    and fathomless as myself,
(They do not know how immortal, but I know.)

Every kind for itself and its own, for me mine male and female,
For me those that have been boys and that love women,   140
For me the man that is proud and feels how it stings to be
    slighted,
For me the sweet-heart and the old maid, for me mothers and
    the mothers of mothers,
For me lips that have smiled, eyes that have shed tears,
For me children and the begetters of children.

Undrape! you are not guilty to me, nor stale nor discarded,
I see through the broadcloth and gingham whether or no,
And am around, tenacious, acquisitive, tireless, and cannot
    be shaken away.

8

The little one sleeps in its cradle,
I lift the gauze and look a long time, and silently brush away
    flies with my hand.
The youngster and the red-faced girl turn aside up the busy
    hill,   150
I peeringly view them from the top.

The suicide sprawls on the bloody floor of the bedroom,

I witness the corpse with its dabbled hair, I note where the
pistol has fallen.

The blab of the pave, tires of carts, sluff of boot-soles, talk of
the promenaders,
The heavy omnibus, the driver with his interrogating thumb,
the clank of the shod horses on the granite floor,
The snow-sleighs, clinking, shouted jokes, pelts of snow-balls,
The hurrahs for popular favorites, the fury of rous'd mobs,
The flap of the curtain'd litter, a sick man inside borne to the
hospital,
The meeting of enemies, the sudden oath, the blows and fall,
The excited crowd, the policeman with his star quickly
working his passage to the centre of the crowd,   160
The impassive stones that receive and return so many echoes,
What groans of over-fed or half-starv'd who fall sunstruck or
in fits,
What exclamations of women taken suddenly who hurry
home and give birth to babes,
What living and buried speech is always vibrating here, what
howls restrain'd by decorum,
Arrests of criminals, slights, adulterous offers made, accept-
ances, rejections with convex lips,
I mind them or the show or resonance of them – I come and
I depart.

11

Twenty-eight young men bathe by the shore,
Twenty-eight young men and all so friendly;   200
Twenty-eight years of womanly life and all so lonesome.

She owns the fine house by the rise of the bank,
She hides handsome and richly drest aft the blinds of the
window.

Which of the young men does she like the best?
Ah the homeliest of them is beautiful to her.

Where are you off to, lady? for I see you,

You splash in the water there, yet stay stock still in your
    room.

Dancing and laughing along the beach came the twenty-
    ninth bather,
The rest did not see her, but she saw them and loved them.

The beards of the young men glisten'd with wet, it ran from
    their long hair,   210
Little streams pass'd all over their bodies.

An unseen hand also pass'd over their bodies,
It descended tremblingly from their temples and ribs.

The young men float on their backs, their white bellies bulge
    to the sun, they do not ask who seizes fast to them,
They do not know who puffs and declines with pendant and
    bending arch,
They do not think whom they souse with spray.

                               15
The pure contralto sings in the organ loft,
The carpenter dresses his plank, the tongue of his foreplane
    whistles its wild ascending lisp,
The married and unmarried children ride home to their
    Thanksgiving dinner,
The pilot seizes the king-pin, he heaves down with a strong
    arm,
The mate stands braced in the whale-boat, lance and
    harpoon are ready,
The duck-shooter walks by silent and cautious stretches,
The deacons are ordain'd with cross'd hands at the altar,   270
The spinning-girl retreats and advances to the hum of the big
    wheel,
The farmer stops by the bars as he walks on a First-day loafe
    and looks at the oats and rye,
The lunatic is carried at last to the asylum a confirm'd case,
(He will never sleep any more as he did in the cot in his
    mother's bedroom;)

The jour printer with gray head and gaunt jaws works at his
    case,
He turns his quid of tobacco while his eyes blurr with the
    manuscript;
The malform'd limbs are tied to the surgeon's table,
What is removed drops horribly in a pail;
The quadroon girl is sold at the auction-stand, the drunkard
    nods by the bar-room stove,
The machinist rolls up his sleeves, the policeman travels his
    beat, the gate-keeper marks who pass,   280
The young fellow drives the express-wagon, (I love him,
    though I do not know him;)
The half-breed straps on his light boots to compete in the race,
The western turkey-shooting draws old and young, some
    lean on their rifles, some sit on logs,
Out from the crowd steps the marksman, takes his position,
    levels his piece;
The groups of newly-come immigrants cover the wharf or
    levee,
As the woolly-pates hoe in the sugar-field, the overseer views
    them from his saddle,
The bugle calls in the ball-room, the gentlemen run for their
    partners, the dancers bow to each other,
The youth lies awake in the cedar-roof'd garret and harks to
    the musical rain,
The Wolverine sets traps on the creek that helps fill the
    Huron,
The squaw wrapt in her yellow-hemm'd cloth is offering
    moccasins and bead-bags for sale,   290
The connoisseur peers along the exhibition-gallery with half-
    shut eyes bent sideways,
As the deck-hands make fast the steamboat the plank is
    thrown for the shore-going passengers,
The young sister holds out the skein while the elder sister
    winds it off in a ball, and stops now and then for the knots,
The one-year wife is recovering and happy having a week ago
    borne her first child,
The clean-hair'd Yankee girl works with her sewing-machine
    or in the factory or mill,
The paving-man leans on his two-handed rammer, the

reporter's lead flies swiftly over the note-book, the sign-
painter is lettering with blue and gold,

The canal boy trots on the tow-path, the book-keeper counts
at his desk, the shoemaker waxes his thread,

The conductor beats time for the band and all the performers
follow him,

The child is baptized, the convert is making his first profes-
sions,

The regatta is spread on the bay, the race is begun, (how the
white sails sparkle!)   300

The drover watching his drove sings out to them that would
stray,

The pedler sweats with his pack on his back, (the purchaser
higgling about the odd cent;)

The bride unrumples her white dress, the minute-hand of the
clock moves slowly,

The opium-eater reclines with rigid head and just-open'd lips,

The prostitute draggles her shawl, her bonnet bobs on her
tipsy and pimpled neck,

The crowd laugh at her blackguard oaths, the men jeer and
wink to each other,

(Miserable! I do not laugh at your oaths nor jeer you;)

The President holding a cabinet council is surrounded by the
great Secretaries,

On the piazza walk three matrons stately and friendly with
twined arms,

The crew of the fish-smack pack repeated layers of halibut in
the hold,   310

The Missourian crosses the plains toting his wares and his
cattle,

As the fare-collector goes through the train he gives notice by
the jingling of loose change,

The floor-men are laying the floor, the tinners are tinning the
roof, the masons are calling for mortar,

In single file each shouldering his hod pass onward the
laborers;

Seasons pursuing each other the indescribable crowd is
gather'd, it is the fourth of Seventh-month, (what salutes
of cannon and small arms!)

Seasons pursuing each other the plougher ploughs, the
    mower mows, the winter-grain falls in the ground;
Off on the lakes the pike-fisher watches and waits by the hole
    in the frozen surface,
The stumps stand thick round the clearing, the squatter
    strikes deep with his axe,
Flatboatmen make fast towards dusk near the cotton-wood or
    pecan-trees,
Coon-seekers go through the regions of the Red river or
    through those drain'd by the Tennessee, or through those
    of the Arkansas,   320
Torches shine in the dark that hangs on the Chattahooche or
    Altamahaw,
Patriarchs sit at supper with sons and grandsons and great-
    grandsons around them.
In walls of adobie, in canvas tents, rest hunters and trappers
    after their day's sport,
The city sleeps and the country sleeps,
The living sleep for their time, the dead sleep for their time,
The old husband sleeps by his wife and the young husband
    sleeps by his wife;
And these tend inward to me, and I tend outward to them,
And such as it is to be of these more or less I am,
And of these one and all I weave the song of myself.

17

These are really the thoughts of all men in all ages and lands,
    they are not original with me,
If they are not yours as much as mine they are nothing, or
    next to nothing,
If they are not the riddle and the untying of the riddle they are
    nothing,
If they are not just as close as they are distant they are
    nothing.

This is the grass that grows wherever the land is and the
    water is,
This is the common air that bathes the globe.

24

Walt Whitman, a kosmos, of Manhattan the son,
Turbulent, fleshy, sensual, eating, drinking and breeding,
No sentimentalist, no stander above men and women or
    apart from them,
No more modest than immodest.   500

Unscrew the locks from the doors!
Unscrew the doors themselves from their jambs!
Whoever degrades another degrades me,
And whatever is done or said returns at last to me.

Through me the afflatus surging and surging, through me
    the current and index.

I speak the pass-word primeval, I give the sign of democracy,
By God! I will accept nothing which all cannot have their
    counterpart of on the same terms.

Through me many long dumb voices,
Voices of the interminable generations of prisoners and
    slaves,
Voices of the diseas'd and despairing and of thieves and
    dwarfs,   510
Voices of cycles of preparation and accretion,
And of the threads that connect the stars, and of wombs and
    of the father-stuff,
And of the rights of them the others are down upon,
Of the deform'd, trivial, flat, foolish, despised,
Fog in the air, beetles rolling balls of dung.

Through me forbidden voices,
Voices of sexes and lusts, voices veil'd and I remove the veil,
Voices indecent by me clarified and transfigur'd.

I do not press my fingers across my mouth,
I keep as delicate around the bowels as around the head and
    heart,   520
Copulation is no more rank to me than death is.

I believe in the flesh and the appetites,

Seeing, hearing, feeling, are miracles, and each part and tag
    of me is a miracle.
Divine am I inside and out, and I make holy whatever I touch
    or am touch'd from,
The scent of these arm-pits aroma finer than prayer,
This head more than churches, bibles, and all the creeds.

If I worship one thing more than another it shall be the spread
    of my own body, or any part of it,
Translucent mould of me it shall be you!
Shaded ledges and rests it shall be you!
Firm masculine colter it shall be you!   530
Whatever goes to the tilth of me it shall be you!
You my rich blood! your milky stream pale strippings of my
    life!
Breast that presses against other breasts it shall be you!
My brain it shall be your occult convolutions!
Root of wash'd sweet-flag! timorous pond-snipe! nest of
    guarded duplicate eggs! it shall be you!
Mix'd tussled hay of head, beard, brawn, it shall be you!
Trickling sap of maple, fibre of manly wheat, it shall be you!
Sun so generous it shall be you!
Vapors lighting and shading my face it shall be you!
You sweaty brooks and dews it shall be you!   540
Winds whose soft-tickling genitals rub against me it shall be
    you!
Broad muscular fields, branches of live oak, loving lounger in
    my winding paths, it shall be you!
Hands I have taken, face I have kiss'd, mortal I have ever
    touch'd, it shall be you.

I dote on myself, there is that lot of me and all so luscious,
Each moment and whatever happens thrills me with joy,
I cannot tell how my ankles bend, nor whence the cause of
    my faintest wish,
Nor the cause of the friendship I emit, nor the cause of the
    friendship I take again.

That I walk up my stoop, I pause to consider if it really be,

A morning-glory at my window satisfies me more than the
     metaphysics of books.

To behold the day-break!   550
The little light fades the immense and diaphanous shadows,
The air tastes good to my palate.

Hefts of the moving world at innocent gambols silently rising,
     freshly exuding,
Scooting obliquely high and low.

Something I cannot see puts upward libidinous prongs,
Seas of bright juice suffuse heaven.
The earth by the sky staid with, the daily close of their
     junction,
The heav'd challenge from the east that moment over my
     head,
The mocking taunt, See then whether you shall be master!

25

Dazzling and tremendous how quick the sun-rise would kill
     me,   560
If I could not now and always send sun-rise out of me.

We also ascend dazzling and tremendous as the sun,
We found our own O my soul in the calm and cool of the
     daybreak.

My voice goes after what my eyes cannot reach,
With the twirl of my tongue I encompass worlds and volumes
     of worlds.

Speech is the twin of my vision, it is unequal to measure itself,
It provokes me forever, it says sarcastically,
Walt you contain enough, why don't you let it out then?

Come now I will not be tantalized, you conceive too much of
     articulation,
Do you not know O speech how the buds beneath you are
     folded?   570

Waiting in gloom, protected by frost,
The dirt receding before my prophetical screams,
I underlying causes to balance them at last,
My knowledge my live parts, it keeping tally with the
    meaning of all things,
Happiness, (which whoever hears me let him or her set out in
    search of this day.)

My final merit I refuse you, I refuse putting from me what I
    really am,
Encompass worlds, but never try to encompass me,
I crowd your sleekest and best by simply looking toward you.

Writing and talk do not prove me,
I carry the plenum of proof and every thing else in my face,   580
With the hush of my lips I wholly confound the skeptic.

27

To be in any form, what is that?
(Round and round we go, all of us, and ever come back
    thither,)
If nothing lay more develop'd the quahaug in its callous shell
    were enough.

Mine is no callous shell,
I have instant conductors all over me whether I pass or stop,
They seize every object and lead it harmlessly through me.

I merely stir, press, feel with my fingers, and am happy,
To touch my person to some one else's is about as much as I
    can stand.

28

Is this then a touch? quivering me to a new identity,
Flames and ether making a rush for my veins,   620
Treacherous tip of me reaching and crowding to help them,
My flesh and blood playing out lightning to strike what is
    hardly different from myself,
On all sides prurient provokers stiffening my limbs,

Straining the udder of my heart for its withheld drip,
Behaving licentious toward me, taking no denial,
Depriving me of my best as for a purpose,
Unbuttoning my clothes, holding me by the bare waist,
Deluding my confusion with the calm of the sunlight and
    pasture-fields,
Immodestly sliding the fellow-senses away,
They bribed to swap off with touch and go and graze at the
    edges of me,   630
No consideration, no regard for my draining strength or my
    anger,
Fetching the rest of the herd around to enjoy them a while,
Then all uniting to stand on a headland and worry me.

The sentries desert every other part of me,
They have left me helpless to a red marauder,
They all come to the headland to witness and assist against
    me.

I am given up by traitors,
I talk wildly, I have lost my wits, I and nobody else am the
    greatest traitor,
I went myself first to the headland, my own hands carried me
    there.

You villain touch! what are you doing? my breath is tight in
    its throat,   640
Unclench your floodgates, you are too much for me.

29

Blind loving wrestling touch, sheath'd hooded sharp-tooth'd
    touch!
Did it make you ache so, leaving me?
Parting track'd by arriving, perpetual payment of perpetual
    loan,
Rich showering rain, and recompense richer afterward.

Sprouts take and accumulate, stand by the curb prolific and
    vital,

Landscapes projected masculine, full-sized and golden.

33

Space and Time! now I see it is true, what I guess'd at, 710
What I guess'd when I loaf'd on the grass,
What I guess'd while I lay alone in my bed,
And again as I walk'd the beach under the paling stars of the
    morning.
My ties and ballasts leave me, my elbows rest in sea-gaps,
I skirt sierras, my palms cover continents,
I am afoot with my vision.
By the city's quadrangular houses – in log huts, camping
    with lumbermen,
Along the ruts of the turnpike, along the dry gulch and rivulet
    bed,
Weeding my onion-patch or hoeing rows of carrots and
    parsnips, crossing savannas, trailing in forests,
Prospecting, gold-digging, girdling the trees of a new pur-
    chase, 720
Scorch'd ankle-deep by the hot sand, hauling my boat down
    the shallow river,
Where the panther walks to and fro on a limb overhead,
    where the buck turns furiously at the hunter,
Where the rattlesnake suns his flabby length on a rock, where
    the otter is feeding on fish,
Where the alligator in his tough pimples sleeps by the bayou,
Where the black bear is searching for roots or honey, where
    the beaver pats the mud with his paddle-shaped tail;
Over the growing sugar, over the yellow-flower'd cotton
    plant, over the rice in its low moist field,
Over the sharp-peak'd farm house, with its scallop'd scum
    and slender shoots from the gutters,
Over the western persimmon, over the long-leav'd corn, over
    the delicate blue-flower flax,
Over the white and brown buckwheat, a hummer and buzzer
    there with the rest,
Over the dusky green of the rye as it ripples and shades in the
    breeze; 730
Scaling mountains, pulling myself cautiously up, holding on
    by low scragged limbs.

Walking the path worn in the grass and beat through the
  leaves of the brush,
Where the quail is whistling betwixt the woods and the
  wheat-lot,
Where the bat flies in the Seventh-month eve, where the
  great gold-bug drops through the dark,
Where the brook puts out of the roots of the old tree and flows
  to the meadow,
Where cattle stand and shake away flies with the tremulous
  shuddering of their hides,
Where the cheese-cloth hangs in the kitchen, where andirons
  straddle the hearth-slab, where cobwebs fall in festoons
  from the rafters;
Where trip-hammers crash, where the press is whirling its
  cylinders.
Where the human heart beats with terrible throes under its
  ribs,
Where the pear-shaped balloon is floating aloft, (floating in it
  myself and looking composedly down,)   740
Where the life-car is drawn on the slip-noose, where the heat
  hatches pale-green eggs in the dented sand,
Where the she-whale swims with her calf and never forsakes
  it,
Where the steam-ship trails hind-ways its long pennant of
  smoke,
Where the fin of the shark cuts like a black chip out of the
  water,
Where the half-burn'd brig is riding on unknown currents,
Where shells grow to her slimy deck, where the dead are
  corrupting below;
Where the dense-starr'd flag is borne at the head of the
  regiments,
Approaching Manhattan up by the long-stretching island,
Under Niagara, the cataract falling like a veil over my coun-
  tenance,
Upon a door-step, upon the horse-block of hard wood outside,   750
Upon the race-course, or enjoying picnics or jigs or a good
  game of base-ball,
At he-festivals, with blackguard gibes, ironical license, bull-
  dances, drinking, laughter,

At the cider-mill tasting the streets of the brown mash,
  sucking the juice through a straw,
At apple-peelings wanting kisses for all the red fruit I find,
At musters, beach-parties, friendly bees, huskings, house-
  raisings;
Where the mocking-bird sounds his delicious gurgles,
  cackles, screams, weeps,
Where the hay-rick stands in the barn-yard, where the dry-
  stalks are scatter'd, where the brood-cow waits in the
  hovel,
Where the bull advances to do his masculine work, where the
  stud to the mare, where the cock is treading the hen,
Where the heifers browse, where geese nip their food with
  short jerks,
Where sun-down shadows lengthen over the limitless and
  lonesome prairie,   760
Where herds of buffalo make a crawling spread of the square
  miles far and near,
Where the humming-bird shimmers, where the neck of the
  long-lived swan is curving and winding,
Where the laughing-gull scoots by the shore, where she
  laughs her near-human laugh,
Where bee-hives range on a gray bench in the garden half hid
  by the high weeds,
Where band-neck'd partridges roost in a ring on the ground
  with their heads out,
Where burial coaches enter the arch'd gates of a cemetery,
Where winter wolves bark amid wastes of snow and icicled
  trees,
Where the yellow-crown'd heron comes to the edge of the
  marsh at night and feeds upon small crabs,
Where the splash of swimmers and divers cools the warm
  noon,
Where the katy-did works her chromatic reed on the walnut-
  tree over the well,   770
Through patches of citrons and cucumbers with silver-wired
  leaves,
Through the salt-lick or orange glade, or under conical firs,
Through the gymnasium, through the curtain'd saloon,
  through the office or public hall;

Pleas'd with the native and pleas'd with the foreign, pleas'd
    with the new and old,
Pleas'd with the homely woman as well as the handsome,
Pleas'd with the quakeress as she puts off her bonnet and talks
    melodiously,
Pleas'd with the tune of the choir of the whitewash'd church,
Pleas'd with the earnest words of the sweating Methodist
    preacher, impress'd seriously at the camp-meeting;
Looking in at the shop-windows of Broadway the whole
    forenoon, flatting the flesh of my nose on the thick plate
    glass,
Wandering the same afternoon with my face turn'd up to the
    clouds, or down a lane or along the beach,   780
My right and left arms round the sides of two friends, and I
    in the middle;
Coming home with the silent and dark-cheek's bush-boy,
    (behind me he rides at the drape of the day,)
Far from the settlements studying the print of animals' feet, or
    the moccasin print,
By the cot in the hospital reaching lemonade to a feverish
    patient,
Nigh the coffin'd corpse when all is still, examining with a
    candle;
Voyaging to every port to dicker and adventure,
Hurrying with the modern crowd as eager and flickle as any,
Hot toward one I hate, ready in my madness to knife him,
Solitary at midnight in my back yard, my thoughts gone from
    me a long while,
Walking the old hills of Judaea with the beautiful gentle God
    by my side,   790
Speeding through space, speeding through heaven and the
    stars,
Speeding amid the seven satellites and the broad ring, and the
    diameter of eighty thousand miles,
Speeding with tail'd meteors, throwing fire-balls like the rest,
Carrying the crescent child that carries its own full mother in
    its belly,
Storming, enjoying, planning, loving, cautioning,
Backing and filling, appearing and disappearing,
I tread day and night such roads.

*

I visit the orchards of spheres and look at the product,
And look at quintillions ripen'd and look at quintillions green.

I fly those flights of a fluid and swallowing soul,   800
My course runs below the soundings of plummets.

I help myself to material and immaterial,
No guard can shut me off, no law prevent me.

I anchor my ship for a little while only,
My messengers continually cruise away or bring their
    returns to me.

I go hunting polar furs and the seal, leaping chasms with a
    pike-pointed staff, clinging to topples of brittle and blue.

I ascend to the foretruck,
I take my place late at night in the crow's-nest,
We sail the arctic sea, it is plenty light enough,
Through the clear atmosphere I stretch around on the
    wonderful beauty,   810
The enormous masses of ice pass me and I pass them, the
    scenery is plain in all directions,
The white-topt mountains show in the distance, I fling out my
    fancies toward them,
We are approaching some great battle-field in which we are
    soon to be engaged,
We pass the colossal outposts of the encampment, we pass
    with still feet and caution,
Or we are entering by the suburbs some vast and ruin'd city,
The blocks and fallen architecture more than all the living
    cities of the globe.

I am a free companion, I bivouac by invading watchfires,
I turn the bridegroom out of bed and stay with the bride
    myself,
I tighten her all night to my thighs and lips.

My voice is the wife's voice, the screech by the rail of the
    stairs,   820
They fetch my man's body up dripping and drown'd.

*

I understand the large hearts of heroes,
The courage of present times and all times,
How the skipper saw the crowded and rudderless wreck of the
    steam-ship, and Death chasing it up and down the storm,
How he knuckled tight and gave not back an inch, and was
    faithful of days and faithful of nights,
And chalk'd in large letters on a board, *Be of good cheer, we will
    not desert you*;
How he follow'd with them and tack'd with them three days
    and would not give it up,
How he saved the drifting company at last,
How the lank loose-gown'd women look'd when boated from
    the side of their prepared graves,
How the silent old-faced infants and the lifted sick, and the
    sharp-lipp'd unshaved men;   830
All this I swallow, it tastes good, I like it well, it becomes mine,
I am the man, I suffer'd, I was there.

The disdain and calmness of martyrs,
The mother of old, condemn'd for a witch, burnt with dry
    wood, her children gazing on,
The hounded slave that flags in the race, leans by the fence,
    blowing, cover'd with sweat,
The twinges that sting like needles his legs and neck, the
    murderous buckshot and the bullets,
All these I feel or am.

I am the hounded slave, I wince at the bite of the dogs,
Hell and despair are upon me, crack and again crack the
    marksmen,
I clutch the rails of the fence, my gore dribs, thinn'd with the
    ooze of my skin,   840
I fall on the weeds and stones,
The riders spur their unwilling horses, haul close,
Taunt my dizzy ears and beat me violently over the head with
    whipstocks.

Agonies are one of my changes of garments,
I do not ask the wounded person how he feels, I myself
    become the wounded person,

My hurts turn livid upon me as I lean on a cane and observe.

I am the mash'd fireman with breast-bone broken,
Tumbling walls buried me in their debris,
Heat and smoke I inspired, I heard the yelling shouts of my
    comrades,
I heard the distant click of their picks and shovels,   850
They have clear'd the beams away, they tenderly lift me forth.
I lie in the night air in my red shirt, the pervading hush is for
    my sake,
Painless after all I lie exhausted but not so unhappy,
White and beautiful are the faces around me, the heads are
    bared of their fire-caps,
The kneeling crowd fades with the light of the torches.
Distant and dead resuscitate,
They show as the dial or move as the hands of me, I am the
    clock myself.

I am an old artillerist, I tell of my fort's bombardment,
I am there again.
Again the long roll of the drummers,   860
Again the attacking cannon, mortars,
Again to my listening ears the cannon responsive.

I take part, I see and hear the whole,
The cries, curses, roar, the plaudits for well-aim'd shots,
The ambulanza slowly passing trailing its red drip,
Workmen searching after damages, making indispensable
    repairs.
The fall of grenades through the rent roof, the fan-shaped
    explosion,
The whizz of limbs, heads, stone, wood, iron, high in the air.

Again gurgles the mouth of my dying general, he furiously
    waves with his hand.
He gasps through the clot *Mind not me – mind – the*
entrenchments.   870

48
I have said that the soul is not more than the body,

And I have said that the body is not more than the soul,   1270
And nothing, not God, is greater to one than one's self is,
And whoever walks a furlong without sympathy walks to his
     own funeral drest in his shroud,
And I or you pocketless of a dime may purchase the pick of the
     earth,
And to glance with an eye or show a bean in its pod
     confounds the learning of all times,
And there is no trade or employment but the young man
     following it may become a hero,
And there is no object so soft but it makes a hub for the
     wheel'd universe,
And I say to any man or woman, Let your soul stand cool and
     composed before a million universes.

And I say to mankind, Be not curious about God,
For I who am curious about each am not curious about God,
(No array of terms can say how much I am at peace about
     God and about death.)   1280

I hear and behold God in every object, yet understand God not
     in the least,
Nor do I understand who there can be more wonderful than
     myself.
Why should I wish to see God better than this day?
I see something of God each hour of the twenty-four, and
     each moment then,
In the faces of men and women I see God, and in my own face
     in the glass,
I find letters from God dropt in the street, and every one is
     sign'd by God's name,
And I leave them where they are, for I know that wheresoe'er
     I go,
Others will punctually come for ever and ever.

49

And as to you, Death, and you bitter hug of mortality, it is idle
     to try to alarm me.

To his work without flinching the accoucheur comes,   1290

I see the elder-hand pressing receiving supporting,
I recline by the sills of the exquisite flexible doors,
And mark the outlet, and mark the relief and escape.

And as to you Corpse I think you are good manure, but that
    does not offend me,
I smell the white roses sweet-scented and growing,
I reach to the leafy lips, I reach to the polish'd breasts of
    melons.
And as to you Life I reckon you are the leavings of many
    deaths,
(No doubt I have died myself ten thousand times before.)

I hear you whispering there O stars of heaven,
O suns – O grass of graves – O perpetual transfers and
    promotions,   1300
If you do not say any thing how can I say any thing?

Of the turbid pool that lies in the autumn forest,
Of the moon that descends the steeps of the soughing twilight,
Toss, sparkles of day and dusk – toss on the black stems that
    decay in the muck,
Toss to the moaning gibberish of the dry limbs.
I ascend from the moon, I ascend from the night,
I perceive that the ghastly glimmer is noonday sunbeams
    reflected,
And debouch to the steady and central from the offspring
    great or small.

50

There is that in me – I do not know what it is – but I know it is
    in me.

Wrench'd and sweaty – calm and cool then my body
    becomes,   1310
I sleep – I sleep long.

I do not know it – it is without name – it is a word unsaid,
It is not in any dictionary, utterance, symbol.

*

Something it swings on more than the earth I swing on,
To it the creation is the friend whose embracing awakes me.

Perhaps I might tell more. Outlines! I plead for my brothers
    and sisters.

Do you see O my brothers and sisters?
It is not chaos or death – it is form, union, plan – it is eternal
    life – it is Happiness.

51

The past and present wilt – I have fill'd them, emptied them,
And proceed to fill my next fold of the future.   1320
Listener up there! what have you to confide to me?
Look in my face while I snuff the sidle of evening,
(Talk honestly, no one else hears you, and I stay only a
    minute longer.)

Do I contradict myself?
Very well then I contradict myself,
(I am large, I contain multitudes.)

I concentrate toward them that are nigh, I wait on the door-
    slab.
Who has done his day's work? who will soonest be through
    with his supper?
Who wishes to walk with me?

Will you speak before I am gone? will you prove already too
    late?   1330

52

The spotted hawk swoops by and accuses me, he complains of
    my gab and my loitering.

I too am not a bit tamed, I too am untranslatable,
I sound my barbaric yawp over the roofs of the world.

The last scud of day holds back for me,
It flings my likeness after the rest and true as any on the

shadow'd wilds,
It coaxes me to the vapor and the dusk.

I depart as air, I shake my white locks at the runaway sun,
I effuse my flesh in eddies, and drift it in lacy jags.

I bequeath myself to the dirt to grow from the grass I love,
If you want me again look for me under your boot-soles.   1340

You will hardly know who I am or what I mean,
But I shall be good health to you nevertheless,
And filter and fibre your blood.

Failing to fetch me at first keep encouraged,
Missing me one place search another,
I stop somewhere waiting for you.

      1855   1881

A Song for Occupations

1

A song for occupations!
In the labor of engines and trades and the labor of fields I find
     the developments,
And find the eternal meanings.

Workmen and Workwomen!
Were all educations practical and ornamental well display'd
     out of me, what would it amount to?
Were I as the head teacher, charitable proprietor, wise
     statesman, what would it amount to?
Were I to you as the boss employing and paying you, would
     that satisfy you?

The learn'd, virtuous, benevolent, and the usual terms,

A man like me and never the usual terms.

Neither a servant nor a master I,   10
I take no sooner a large price than a small price, I will have
    my own whoever enjoys me,
I will be even with you and you shall be even with me.

If you stand at work in a shop I stand as nigh as the nighest in
    the same shop,
If you bestow gifts on your brother or dearest friend I demand
    as good as your brother or dearest friend,
If your lover, husband, wife, is welcome by day or night, I
    must be personally as welcome,
If you become degraded, criminal, ill, then I become so for
    your sake,
If you remember your foolish and outlaw'd deeds, do you
    think I cannot remember my own foolish and outlaw'd
    deeds?
If you carouse at the table I carouse at the opposite side of the
    table,
If you meet some stranger in the streets and love him or her,
    why I often meet strangers in the street and love them.

Why what have you thought of yourself?   20
Is it you then that thought yourself less?
Is it you that thought the President greater than you?
Or the rich better off than you? or the educated wiser than
    you?
(Because you are greasy or pimpled, or were once drunk, or a
    thief,
Or that you are diseas'd, or rheumatic, or a prostitute,
Or from frivolity or impotence, or that you are no scholar and
    never saw your name in print,
Do you give in that you are any less immortal?)

2

Souls of men and women! it is not you I call unseen, unheard,
    untouchable and untouching,
It is not you I go argue pro and con about, and to settle
    whether you are alive or no,

I own publicly who you are, if nobody else owns.   30

Grown, half-grown and babe, of this country and every
    country, indoors, and out-doors, one just as much as the
    other, I see,
And all else behind or through them.

The wife, and she is not one jot less than the husband,
The daughter, and she is just as good as the son,
The mother, and she is every bit as much as the father.

Offspring of ignorant and poor, boys apprenticed to trades,
Young fellows working on farms and old fellows working on
    farms,
Sailor-men, merchant-men, coasters, immigrants,
All these I see, but nigher and farther the same I see,
None shall escape me and none shall wish to escape me.   40

I bring what you much need yet always have,
Not money, amours, dress, eating, erudition, but as good,
I send no agent or medium, offer no representative of value,
    but offer the value itself.

There is something that comes to one now and perpetually,
It is not what is printed, preach'd, discussed, it eludes
    discussion and print,
It is not to be put in a book, it is not in this book,
It is for you whoever you are, it is no farther from you than
    your hearing and sight are from you,
It is hinted by nearest, commonest, readiest, it is ever
    provoked by them.
You may read in many languages, yet read nothing about it,
You may read the President's message and read nothing
    about it there,   50
Nothing in the reports from the State department or Treasury
    department, or in the daily papers or weekly papers,
Or in the census or revenue returns, prices current, or any
    accounts of stock.

3

The sun and stars that float in the open air,

The apple-shaped earth and we upon it, surely the drift of them is something grand,

I do not know what it is except that it is grand, and that it is happiness,

And that the enclosing purport of us here is not a speculation or bon-mot or reconnoissance,

And that it is not something which by luck may turn out well for us, and without luck must be a failure for us,

And not something which may yet be retracted in a certain contingency.

The light and shade, the curious sense of body and identity, the greed that with perfect complaisance devours all things,

The endless pride and outstretching of man, unspeakable joys and sorrows,   60

The wonder every one sees in every one else he sees, and the wonders that fill each minute of time forever,

What have you reckon'd them for, camerado?

Have you reckon'd them for your trade or farm-work? or for the profits of your store?

Or to achieve yourself a position? or to fill a gentleman's leisure, or a lady's leisure?

Have you reckon'd that the landscape took substance and form that it might be painted in a picture?

Or men and women that they might be written of, and songs sung?

Or the attraction of gravity, and the great laws and harmonious combinations and the fluids of the air, as subjects for the savans?

Or the brown land and the blue sea for maps and charts?

Or the stars to be put in constellations and named fancy names?

Or that the growth of seeds is for agricultural tables, or agriculture itself?   70

Old institutions, these arts, libraries, legends, collections, and

the practice handed along in manufactures, will we rate
them so high?
Will we rate our cash and business high? I have no objection,
I rate them as high as the highest – then a child born of a
woman and man I rate beyond all rate.

We thought our Union grand, and our Constitution grand,
I do not say they are not grand and good, for they are,
I am this day just as much in love with them as you,
Then I am in love with You, and with all my fellows upon the
earth.

We consider bibles and religions divine – I do not say they are
not divine,
I say they have all grown out of you, and may grow out of you
still,
It is not they who give the life, it is you who give the life,   80
Leaves are not more shed from the trees, or trees from the
earth, than they are shed out of you.

4

The sum of all known reverence I add up in you whoever you
are,
The President is there in the White House for you, it is not you
who are here for him,
The Secretaries act in their bureaus for you, not you here for
them,
The Congress convenes every Twelfth-month for you,
Laws, courts, the forming of States, the charters of cities, the
going and coming of commerce and mails, are all for you.

List close my scholars dear,
Doctrines, politics and civilization exurge from you,
Sculpture and monuments and any thing inscribed any-
where are tallied in you,
The gist of histories and statistics as far back as the records
reach is in you this hour, and myths and tales the same,   90
If you were not breathing and walking here, where would
they all be?

The most renown'd poems would be ashes, orations and plays
    would be vacuums.

All architecture is what you do to it when you look upon it,
(Did you think it was in the white or gray stone? or the lines of
    the arches and cornices?)
All music is what awakes from you when you are reminded
    by the instruments,
It is not the violins and the cornets, it is not the oboe nor the
    beating drums, nor the score of the baritone singer singing
    his sweet romanza, nor that of the men's chorus, nor that
    of the women's chorus.
It is nearer and farther than they.

5

Will the whole come back then?
Can each see signs of the best by a look in the looking-glass? is
    there nothing greater or more?
Does all sit there with you, with the mystic unseen soul?   100

Strange and hard that paradox true I give,
Objects gross and the unseen soul are one.

House-building, measuring, sawing the boards,
Blacksmithing, glass-blowing, nail-making, coopering, tin-
    roofing, shingle-dressing,
Ship-joining, dock-building, fish-curing, flagging of side-
    walks by flaggers,
The pump, the pile-driver, the great derrick, the coal-kiln and
    brick-kiln,
Coal-mines and all that is down there, the lamps in the
    darkness, echoes, songs, what meditations, what vast
    native thoughts looking through smutch'd faces,
Iron-works, forge-fires in the mountains or by river-banks,
    men around feeling the melt with huge crowbars, lumps of
    ore, the due combining of ore, limestone, coal,
The blast-furnace and the pudding-furnace, the loup-lump at
    the bottom of the melt at last, the rolling-mill, the stumpy
    bars of pig-iron, the strong, clean-shaped T-rail for
    railroads.

Oil-works, silk-works, white-lead-works, the sugar-house, steam-saws, the great mills and factories,   110

Stone-cutting, shapely trimmings for façades or window or door-lintels, the mallet, the tooth-chisel, the jib to protect the thumb,

The calking-iron, the kettle of boiling vault-cement, and the fire under the kettle,

The cotton-bale, the stevedore's hook, the saw and buck of the sawyer, the mould of the moulder, the working-knife of the butcher, the ice-saw, and all the work with ice,

The work and tools of the rigger, grappler, sail-maker, block-maker,

Goods of gutta-percha, papier-maché, colors, brushes, brush-making, glazier's implements,

The veneer and glue-pot, the confectioner's ornaments, the decanter and glasses, the shears and flat-iron,

The awl and knee-strap, the pint measure and quart measure, the counter and stool, the writing-pen of quill or metal, the making of all sorts of edged tools,

The brewery, brewing, the malt, the vats, everything that is done by brewers, wine-makers, vinegar-makers,

Leather-dressing, coach-making, boiler-making, rope-twisting, distilling, sign-painting, lime-burning, cotton-picking, electroplating, electrotyping, stereotyping,

Stave-machines, planing-machines, reaping-machines, ploughing-machines, thrashing-machines, steam wagons,   120

The cart of the carman, the omnibus, the ponderous dray,

Pyrotechny, letting off color'd fireworks at night, fancy figures and jets;

Beef on the butcher's stall, the slaughter-house of the butcher, the butcher in his killing-clothes,

The pens of live pork, the killing-hammer, the hog-hook, the scalder's tub, gutting, the cutter's cleaver, the packer's maul, and the plenteous winterwork of pork-packing,

Flour-works, grinding of wheat, rye, maize, rice, the barrels and the half and quarter barrels, the loaded barges, the high piles on wharves and levees,

The men and the work of the men on ferries, railroads, coasters, fish-boats, canals;

The hourly routine of your own or any man's life, the shop, yard, store, or factory,
These shows all near you by day and night – workman! whoever you are, your daily life!
In that and them the heft of the heaviest – in that and them far more than you estimated, (and far less also,)
In them realities for you and me, in them poems for you and me,　　　　130
In them, not yourself – you and your soul enclose all things, regardless of estimation,
In them the development good – in them all themes, hints, possibilities.

I do not affirm that what you see beyond is futile, I do not advise you to stop,
I do not say leadings you thought great are not great,
But I say that none lead to greater than these lead to.

6

Will you seek afar off? you surely come back at last,
In things best known to you finding the best, or as good as the best,
In folks nearest to you finding the sweetest, strongest, lovingest,
Happiness, knowledge, not in another place but this place, not for another hour but this hour,
Man in the first you see or touch, always in friend, brother, nighest neighbor – woman in mother, sister, wife,　　　　140
The popular tastes and employments taking precedence in poems or anywhere,
You workwomen and workmen of these States having your own divine and strong life,
And all else giving place to men and women like you.

When the psalm sings instead of the singer,
When the script preaches instead of the preacher,
When the pulpit descends and goes instead of the carver that carved the supporting desk,
When I can touch the body of books by night or by day, and when they touch my body back again,

When a university course convinces like a slumbering
  woman and child convince,
When the minted gold in the vault smiles like the night-
  watchman's daughter,
When warrantee deeds loafe in chairs opposite and are my
  friendly companions,   150
I intend to reach them my hand, and make as much of them
  as I do of men and women like you.

1855   1881

The Sleepers

1

I wander all night in my vision,
Stepping with light feet, swiftly and noiselessly stepping and
  stopping,
Bending with open eyes over the shut eyes of sleepers,
Wandering and confused, lost to myself, ill-assorted, contra-
  dictory,
Pausing, gazing, bending, and stopping.
How solemn they look there, stretch'd and still,
How quiet they breathe, the little children in their cradles.

The wretched features of ennuyés, the white features of
  corpses, the livid faces of drunkards, the sick-gray faces of
  onanists,
The gash'd bodies on battle-fields, the insane in their strong-
  door'd rooms, the sacred idiots, the new-born emerging
  from gates, and the dying emerging from gates,
The night pervades them and infolds them.   10

The married couple sleep calmly in their bed, he with his palm
  on the hip of the wife, and she with her palm on the hip of
  the husband,
The sisters sleep lovingly side by side in their bed,
The men sleep lovingly side by side in theirs,

And the mother sleeps with her little child carefully wrapt.

The blind sleep, and the deaf and dumb sleep,
The prisoner sleeps well in the prison, the runaway son
     sleeps,
The murderer that is to be hung next day, how does he sleep?
And the murder'd person, how does he sleep?

The female that loves unrequited sleeps,
And the male that loves unrequited sleeps,   20
The head of the money-maker that plotted all day sleeps,
And the enraged and treacherous dispositions, all, all sleep.

I stand in the dark with drooping eyes by the worst-suffering
     and the most restless,
I pass my hands soothingly to and fro a few inches from them,
The restless sink in their beds, they fitfully sleep.
Now I pierce the darkness, new beings appear,
The earth recedes from me into the night,
I saw that it was beautiful, and I see that what is not the earth
     is beautiful.

I go from bedside to bedside, I sleep close with the other
     sleepers each in turn,
I dream in my dream all the dreams of the other dreamers,   30
And I become the other dreamers.

I am a dance – play up there! the fit is whirling me fast!
I am the ever-laughing – it is new moon and twilight,
I see the hiding of douceurs, I see nimble ghosts whichever
     way I look,
Cache and cache again deep in the ground and sea, and
     where it is neither ground nor sea.

Well do they do their jobs those journeymen divine,
Only from me can they hide nothing, and would not if they
     could,
I reckon I am their boss and they make me a pet besides,
And surround me and lead me and run ahead when I walk,
To lift their cunning covers to signify me with stretch'd arms,

and resume the way;   40
Onward we move, a gay gang of blackguards! with mirth-
    shouting music and wild-flapping pennants of joy!

I am the actor, the actress, the voter, the politician,
The emigrant and the exile, the criminal that stood in the box,
He who has been famous and he who shall be famous after
    today,
The stammerer, the well-formed person, the wasted or feeble
    person.
I am she who adorn'd herself and folded her hair expectantly,
My truant lover has come, and it is dark.

Double yourself and receive me darkness,
Receive me and my lover too, he will not let me go without
    him.

I roll myself upon you as upon a bed, I resign myself to the
    dusk.   50

He whom I call answers me and takes the place of my lover,
He rises with me silently from the bed.

Darkness, you are gentler than my lover, his flesh was sweaty
    and panting,
I feel the hot moisture yet that he left me.

My hands are spread forth, I pass them in all directions,
I would sound up the shadowy shore to which you are
    journeying.

Be careful darkness! already what was it touch'd me?
I thought my lover had gone, else darkness and he are one,
I hear the heart-beat, I follow, I fade away.

2

I descend my western course, my sinews are flaccid,   60
Perfume and youth course through me and I am their wake.

It is my face yellow and wrinkled instead of the old woman's,

I sit low in a straw-bottom chair and carefully darn my
    grandson's stockings.

It is I too, the sleepless widow looking out on the winter
    midnight,
I see the sparkles of starshine on the icy and pallid earth.

A shroud I see and I am the shroud, I wrap a body and lie in
    the coffin,
It is dark here under ground, it is not evil or pain here, it is
    blank here, for reasons.

(It seems to me that every thing in the light and air ought to
    be happy,
Whoever is not in his coffin and the dark grave let him know
    he has enough.)

3

I see a beautiful gigantic swimmer swimming naked through
    the eddies of the sea,   70
His brown hair lies close and even to his head, he strikes out
    with courageous arms, he urges himself with his legs,
I see his white body, I see his undaunted eyes,
I hate the swift-running eddies that would dash him head-
    foremost on the rocks.

What are you doing you ruffianly red-trickled waves?
Will you kill the courageous giant? will you kill him in the
    prime of his middle age?

Steady and long he struggles,
He is baffled, bang'd, bruis'd, he holds out while his strength
    holds out,
The slapping eddies are spotted with his blood, they bear him
    away, they roll him, swing him, turn him,
His beautiful body is borne in the circling eddies, it is
    continually bruis'd on rocks,
Swiftly and out of sight is borne the brave corpse.   80

4

I turn but do not extricate myself,
Confused, a past-reading, another, but with darkness yet.

The beach is cut by the razory ice-wind, the wreck-guns
    sound,
The tempest lulls, the moon comes floundering through the
    drifts.

I look where the ship helplessly heads end on, I hear the
    burst as she strikes, I hear the howls of dismay, they grow
    fainter and fainter.

I cannot aid with my wringing fingers,
I can but rush to the surf and let it drench me and freeze upon
    me.

I search with the crowd, not one of the company is wash'd to
    us alive,
In the morning I help pick up the dead and lay them in rows in
    a barn.

5

Now of the older war-days, the defeat at Brooklyn,   90
Washington stands inside the lines, he stands on the
    intrench'd hills amid a crowd of officers,
His face is cold and damp, he cannot repress the weeping
    drops,
He lifts the glass perpetually to his eyes, the color is blanch'd
    from his cheeks,
He sees the slaughter of the southern braves confided to him
    by their parents.

The same at last and at last when peace is declared,
He stands in the room of the old tavern, the well-belov'd
    soldiers all pass through,
The officers speechless and slow draw near in their turns,
The chief encircles their necks with his arm and kisses them
    on the cheek,
He kisses lightly the wet-cheeks one after another, he shakes
    hands and bids good-by to the army.

6

Now what my mother told me one day as we sat at dinner
    together,   100
Of when she was a nearly grown girl living home with her
    parents on the old homestead.

A red squaw came one breakfast-time to the old homestead,
On her back she carried a bundle of rushes for rush-
    bottoming chairs,
Her hair, straight, shiny, coarse, black, profuse, half-envel-
    op'd her face,
Her step was free and elastic, and her voice sounded
    exquisitely as she spoke.

My mother looked in delight and amazement at the stranger,
She look'd at the freshness of her tall-borne face and full and
    pliant limbs,
The more she look'd upon her she loved her,
Never before had she seen such wonderful beauty and purity,
She made her sit on a bench by the jamb of the fireplace, she
    cook'd food for her,   110
She had no work to give her, but she gave her remembrance
    and fondness.

The red squaw staid all the forenoon, and toward the middle
    of the afternoon she went away,
O my mother was loth to have her go away,
All the week she thought of her, she watch'd for her many a
    month,
She remember'd her many a winter and many a summer,
But the red squaw never came nor was heard of there again.

7

A show of the summer softness – a contact of something
    unseen – an amour of the light and air,
I am jealous and overwhelm'd with friendliness,
And will go gallivant with the light and air myself.

O love and summer, you are in the dreams and in me,   120
Autumn and winter are in the dreams, the farmer goes with
    his thrift,

The droves and crops increase, the barns are well-fill'd.
Elements merge in the night, ships make tacks in the dreams,
The sailor sails, the exile returns home,
The fugitive returns unharm'd, the immigrant is back beyond
    months and years,
The poor Irishman lives in the simple house of his childhood
    with the well-known neighbors and faces,
They warmly welcome him, he is barefoot again, he forgets
    he is well off,
The Dutchman voyages home, and the Scotchman and
    Welshman voyage home, and the native of the Mediter-
    ranean voyages home,
To every port of England, France, Spain, enter well-fill'd
    ships,
The Swiss foots it toward his hills, the Prussian goes his way,
    the Hungarian his way, and the Pole his way,   130
The Swede returns, and the Dane and Norwegian return.

The homeward bound and the outward bound,
The beautiful lost swimmer, the ennuyé, the onanist, the
    female that loves unrequited, the money-maker,
The actor and actress, those through with their parts and
    those waiting to commence,
The affectionate boy, the husband and wife, the voter, the
    nominee that is chosen and the nominee that has fail'd,
The great already known and the great any time after to-day,
The stammerer, the sick, the perfect-form'd, the homely,
The criminal that stood in the box, the judge that sat and
    sentenced him, the fluent lawyers, the jury, the audience,
The laughter and weeper, the dancer, the midnight widow,
    the red squaw,
The consumptive, the erysipalite, the idiot, he that is
    wrong'd,   140
The antipodes, and every one between this and them in the
    dark,
I swear they are averaged now – one is no better than the
    other,
The night and sleep have liken'd them and restored them.

I swear they are all beautiful,

Every one that sleeps is beautiful, every thing in the dim light
    is beautiful,
The wildest and bloodiest is over, and all is peace.

Peace is always beautiful,
The myth of heaven indicates peace and night.
The myth of heaven indicates the soul,
The soul is always beautiful, it appears more or it appears less,
    it comes or it lags behind,   150
It comes from its embower'd garden and looks pleasantly on
    itself and encloses the world,
Perfect and clean the genitals previously jetting, and perfect
    and clean the womb cohering,
The head well-grown proportion'd and plumb, and the
    bowels and joints proportion'd and plumb.

The soul is always beautiful,
The universe is duly in order, every thing is in its place,
What has arrived is in its place and what waits shall be in its
    place,
The twisted skull waits, the watery or rotten blood waits,
The child of the glutton or venerealee waits long, and the
    child of the drunkard waits long, and the drunkard himself
    waits long,
The sleepers that lived and died wait, the far advanced are to
    go on in their turns, and the far behind are to come on in
    their turns,
The diverse shall be no less diverse, but they shall flow and
    unite – they unite now.   160

8

The sleepers are very beautiful as they lie unclothed,
They flow hand in hand over the whole earth from east to
    west as they lie unclothed,
The Asiatic and African are hand in hand, the European and
    American are hand in hand,
Learn'd and unlearn'd are hand in hand, and male and
    female are hand in hand,
The bare arm of the girl crosses the bare breast of her lover,
    they press close without lust, his lips press her neck,

The father holds his grown or ungrown son in his arms with
   measureless love, and the son holds the father in his arms
   with measureless love,
The white hair of the mother shines on the white wrist of the
   daughter,
The breath of the boy goes with the breath of the man, friend
   is inarm'd by friend,
The scholar kisses the teacher and the teacher kisses the
   scholar, the wrong'd is made right,
The call of the slave is one with the master's call, and the
   master salutes the slave,   170
The felon steps forth from the prison, the insane becomes
   sane, the suffering of sick persons is reliev'd.
The sweating and fevers stop, the throat that was unsound is
   sound, the lungs of the consumptive are resumed, the poor
   distress'd head is free,
The joints of the rheumatic move as smoothly as ever, and
   smoother than ever,
Stiflings and passages open, the paralyzed become supple,
They swell'd and convuls'd and congested awake to them-
   selves in condition,
They pass the invigoration of the night and the chemistry of
   the night, and awake.

I too pass from the night,
I stay a while away O night, but I return to you again and
   love you.

Why should I be afraid to trust myself to you?
I am not afraid, I have been well brought forward by you,   180
I love the rich running day, but I do not desert her in whom I
   lay so long,
I know not how I came of you and I know not where I go with
   you, but I know I came well and shall go well.

I will stop only a time with the night, and rise betimes,
I will duly pass the day O my mother, and duly return to you.

1855   1881

Crossing Brooklyn Ferry

1

Flood-tide below me! I see you face to face!

Clouds of the west – sun there half an hour high – I see you
also face to face.

Crowds of men and women attired in the usual costumes,
how curious you are to me!

On the ferry-boats the hundreds and hundreds that cross,
returning home, are more curious to me than you
suppose,

And you that shall cross from shore to shore years hence are
more to me, and more in my meditations, than you might
suppose.

2

The impalpable sustenance of me from all things at all hours
of the day,

The simple, compact, well-join'd scheme, myself disinte-
grated, every one disintegrated yet part of the scheme,

The similitudes of the past and those of the future,

The glories strung like beads on my smallest sights and
hearings, on the walk in the street and the passage over
the river,

The current rushing so swiftly and swimming with me far
away,

The others that are to follow me, the ties between me and
them,

The certainty of others, the life, love, sight, hearing of others.

Others will enter the gates of the ferry and cross from shore to
shore,

Others will watch the run of the flood-tide,

Others will see the shipping of Manhattan north and west,
and the heights of Brooklyn to the south and east,

Others will see the islands large and small;

Fifty years hence, others will see them as they cross, the sun
half an hour high,

A hundred years hence, or ever so many hundred years hence,
  others will see them,
Will enjoy the sunset, the pouring-in of the flood-tide, the
  falling-back to the sea of the ebb-tide.

3

It avails not, time nor place – distance avails not, 20
I am with you, you men and women of a generation, or ever
  so many generations hence,
Just as you feel when you look on the river and sky, so I felt,
Just as any of you is one of a living crowd, I was one of a
  crowd,
Just as you are refresh'd by the gladness of the river and the
  bright flow, I was refresh'd,
Just as you stand and lean on the rail, yet hurry with the swift
  current, I stood yet was hurried,
Just as you look on the numberless masts of ships and the
  thick-stemm'd pipes of steamboats, I look'd.

I too many and many a time cross'd the river of old,
Watched the Twelfth-month sea-gulls, saw them high in the
  air floating with motionless wings, oscillating their bodies,
Saw how the glistening yellow lit up parts of their bodies and
  left the rest in strong shadow,
Saw the slow-wheeling circles and the gradual edging toward
  the south, 30
Saw the reflection of the summer sky in the water,
Had my eyes dazzled by the shimmering track of beams,
Look'd at the fine centrifugal spokes of light round the shape
  of my head in the sunlit water,
Look'd on the haze on the hills southward and south-
  westward,
Look'd on the vapor as it flew in fleeces tinged with violet,
Look'd toward the lower bay to notice the vessels arriving,
Saw their approach, saw aboard those that were near me,
Saw the white sails of schooners and sloops, saw the ships at
  anchor,
The sailors at work in the rigging or out astride the spars,
The round masts, the swinging motion of the hulls, the
  slender serpentine pennants, 40

The large and small steamers in motion, the pilots in their
    pilot-houses,
The white wake left by the passage, the quick tremulous whirl
    of the wheels,
The flags of all nations, the falling of them at sunset,
The scallop-edged waves in the twilight, the ladled cups, the
    frolicsome crests and glistening,
The stretch afar growing dimmer and dimmer, the gray walls
    of the granite storehouses by the docks,
On the river the shadowy group, the big steam-tug closely
    flank'd on each side by the barges, the hay-boat, the
    belated lighter,
On the neighboring shore the fires from the foundry chim-
    neys burning high and glaringly into the night,
Casting their flicker of black contrasted with wild red and
    yellow light over the tops of houses, and down into the
    clefts of streets.

4

These and all else were to me the same as they are to you,
I loved well those cities, loved well the stately and rapid river,   50
The men and women I saw were all near to me,
Others the same – others who look back on me because I
    look'd forward to them,
(The time will come, though I stop here to-day and to-night.)

5

What is it then between us?
What is the count of the scores or hundreds of years between
    us?

Whatever it is, it avails not – distance avails not, and place
    avails not,
I too lived, Brooklyn of ample hills was mine,
I too walk'd the streets of Manhattan island, and bathed in the
    waters around it,
I too felt the curious abrupt questionings stir within me.
In the day among crowds of people sometimes they came
    upon me,   60

In my walks home late at night or as I lay in my bed they came
    upon me,
I too had been struck from the float forever held in solution,
I too had receiv'd identity by my body,
That I was I knew was of my body, and what I should be I
    knew I should be of my body.

6

It is not upon you alone the dark patches fall,
The dark threw its patches down upon me also,
The best I had done seem'd to me blank and suspicious,
My great thoughts as I supposed them, were they not in
    reality meagre?
Nor is it you alone who know what it is to be evil,
I am he who knew what it was to be evil,   70
I too knitted the old knot of contrariety,
Blabb'd, blush'd, resented, lied, stole, grudg'd,
Had guile, anger, lust, hot wishes I dared not speak,
Was wayward, vain, greedy, shallow, sly, cowardly, malig-
    nant,
The wolf, the snake, the hog, not wanting in me,
The cheating look, the frivolous word, the adulterous wish,
    not wanting,
Refusals, hates, postponements, meanness, laziness, none of
    these wanting,
Was one with the rest, the days and haps of the rest,
Was call'd by my nighest name by clear loud voices of young
    men as they saw me approaching or passing,
Felt their arms on my neck as I stood, or the negligent leaning
    of their flesh against me as I sat,   80
Saw many I loved in the street or ferry-boat or public
    assembly, yet never told them a word,
Lived the same life with the rest, the same old laughing,
    gnawing, sleeping,
Play'd the part that still looks back on the actor or actress,
The same old role, the role that is what we make it, as great as
    we like,
Or as small as we like, or both great and small.

7

Closer yet I approach you,
What thought you have of me now, I had as much of you – I
    laid in my stores in advance,
I consider'd long and seriously of you before you were born.

Who was to know what should come home to me?
Who knows but I am enjoying this?   90
Who knows, for all the distance, but I am as good as looking
    at you now, for all you cannot see me?

8

Ah, what can ever be more stately and admirable to me than
    mast-hemm'd Manhattan?
River and sunset and scallop-edg'd waves of flood-tide?
The sea-gulls oscillating their bodies, the hay-boat in the
    twilight, and the belated lighter?
What gods can exceed these that clasp me by the hand, and
    with voices I love call me promptly and loudly by my
    nighest name as I approach?
What is more subtle than this which ties me to the woman or
    man that looks in my face?
Which fuses me into you now, and pours my meaning into
    you?

We understand then do we not?
What I promis'd without mentioning it, have you not
    accepted?
What the study could not teach – what the preaching could
    not accomplish is accomplish'd, is it not?   100

9

Flow on, river! flow with the flood-tide, and ebb with the ebb-
    tide!
Frolic on, crested and scallop-edg'd waves!
Gorgeous clouds of the sunset! drench with your splendor me,
    or the men and women generations after me!
Cross from shore to shore, countless crowds of passengers!
Stand up, tall masts of Mannahatta! stand up, beautiful hills
    of Brooklyn!

Throb, baffled and curious brain! throw out questions and
  answers!
Suspend here and everywhere, eternal float of solution!
Gaze, loving and thirsting eyes, in the house or street or
  public assembly!
Sound out, voices of young men! loudly and musically call me
  by my nighest name!
Live, old life! play the part that looks back on the actor or
  actress!   110
Play the old role, the role that is great or small according as
  one makes it!
Consider, you who peruse me, whether I may not in
  unknown ways be looking upon you;
Be firm, rail over the river, to support those who lean idly, yet
  haste with the hasting current;
Fly on, sea-birds! fly sideways, or wheel in large circles high in
  the air;
Receive the summer sky, you water, and faithfully hold it till
  all downcast eyes have time to take it from you!
Diverge, fine spokes of light, from the shape of my head, or
  any one's head, in the sunlit water!
Come on, ships from the lower bay! pass up or down, white-
  sail'd schooners, sloops, lighters!
Flaunt away, flags of all nations! be duly lower'd at sunset!
Burn high your fires, foundry chimneys! cast black shadows
  at nightfall! cast red and yellow light over the tops of the
  houses!
Appearances, now or henceforth, indicate what you are,   120
You necessary film, continue to envelop the soul,
About my body for me, and your body for you, be hung our
  divinest aromas,
Thrive, cities – bring your freight, bring your shows, ample
  and sufficient rivers,
Expand, being than which none else is perhaps more
  spiritual,
Keep your places, objects than which none else is more
  lasting,

You have waited, you always wait, you dumb, beautiful
  ministers,
We receive you with free sense at last, and are insatiate
  henceforward,

Not you any more shall be able to foil us, or withhold
    yourselves from us,
We use you, and do not cast you aside – we plant you
    permanently within us,
We fathom you not – we love you – there is perfection in you
    also,   130
Your furnish your parts toward eternity,
Great or small, you furnish your parts toward the soul.

    1856   1881

Out of the Cradle Endlessly Rocking

Out of the cradle endlessly rocking,
Out of the mocking-bird's throat, the musical shuttle,
Out of the Ninth-month midnight,
Over the sterile sands and the fields beyond, where the child
    leaving his bed wander'd alone, bareheaded, barefoot,
Down from the shower'd halo,
Up from the mystic play of shadows twining and twisting as if
    they were alive,
Out from the patches of briers and blackberries,
From the memories of the bird that chanted to me,
From your memories sad brother, from the fitful risings and
    fallings I heard,
From under that yellow half-moon late-risen and swollen as if
    with tears,   10
From those beginning notes of yearning and love there in the
    mist,
From the thousand responses of my heart never to cease,
From the myriad thence-arous'd words,
From the word stronger and more delicious than any,
From such as now they start the scene revisiting,
As a flock, twittering, rising, or overhead passing,
Borne hither, ere all eludes me, hurriedly,
A man, yet by these tears a little boy again,
Throwing myself on the sand, confronting the waves,

I, chanter of pains and joys, uniter of here and hereafter,   20
Taking all hints to use them, but swiftly leaping beyond them,
A reminiscence sing.

Once Paumanok,
When the lilac-scent was in the air and Fifth-month grass
    was growing,
Up this seashore in some briers,
Two feather'd guests from Alabama, two together,
And their nest, and four light-green eggs spotted with brown,
And every day the he-bird to and fro near at hand,
And every day the she-bird crouch'd on her nest, silent, with
    bright eyes,
And every day I, a curious boy, never too close, never
    disturbing them,   30
Cautiously peering, absorbing, translating.

Shine! shine! shine!
Pour down your warmth, great sun!
While we bask, we two together.

Two together!
Winds blow south, or winds blow north,
Day come white, or night come black,
Home, or rivers and mountains from home,
Singing all time, minding no time,
While we two keep together.   40

Till of a sudden,
May-be kill'd, unknown to her mate,
One forenoon the she-bird crouch'd not on the nest,
Nor return'd that afternoon, nor the next,
Nor ever appear'd again.

And thenceforward all summer in the sound of the sea,
And at night under the full of the moon in calmer weather,
Over the hoarse surging of the sea,
Or flitting from brier to brier by day,
I saw, I heard at intervals the remaining one, the he-bird,   50
The solitary guest from Alabama.

Blow! blow! blow!
Blow up sea-winds along Paumanok's shore;
I wait and I wait till you blow my mate to me.

Yes, when the stars glisten'd,
All night long on the prong of a moss-scallop'd stake,
Down almost amid the slapping waves,
Sat the lone singer wonderful causing tears.

He call'd on his mate,
He pour'd forth the meanings which I of all men know.   60

Yes my brother I know,
The rest might not, but I have treasur'd every note,
For more than once dimly down to the beach gliding,
Silent, avoiding the moonbeams, blending myself with the
    shadows,
Recalling now the obscure shapes, the echoes, the sounds
    and sights after their sorts,
The white arms out in the breakers tirelessly tossing,
I, with bare feet, a child, the wind wafting my hair,
Listen'd long and long.

Listen'd to keep, to sing, now translating the notes,
Following you my brother.   70

Soothe! soothe! soothe!
Close on its wave soothes the wave behind,
And again another behind embracing and lapping, every one close,
But my love soothes not me, not me.

Low hangs the moon, it rose late,
It is lagging – O I think it is heavy with love, with love.

O madly the sea pushes upon the land,
With love, with love.

O night! do I not see my love fluttering out among the breakers?
What is that little black thing I see there in the white?   80

*

Loud! loud! loud!
Loud I call to you, my love!
High and clear I shoot my voice over the waves,
Surely you must know who is here, is here,
You must know who I am, my love.

Low-hanging moon!
What is that dusky spot in your brown yellow?
O it is the shape, the shape of my mate!
O moon do not keep her from me any longer.

Land! land! O land!   90
Whichever way I turn, O I think you could give me my mate back
    again if you only would,
For I am almost sure I see her dimly whichever way I look.

O rising stars!
Perhaps the one I want so much will rise, will rise with some of
    you.
O throat! O trembling throat!
Sound clearer through the atmosphere!
Pierce the woods, the earth,
Somewhere listening to catch you must be the one I want.

Shake out carols!
Solitary here, the night's carols!   100
Carols of lonesome love! death's carols!
Carols under that lagging, yellow, waning moon!
O under that moon where she droops almost down into the sea!
O reckless despairing carols.

But soft! sink low!
Soft! let me just murmur,
And do you wait a moment you husky-nois'd sea,
For somewhere I believe I heard my mate responding to me,
So faint, I must be still, be still to listen,
But not altogether still, for then she might not come immediately
    to me.   110

Hither my love!

Here I am! here!
With this just-sustain'd note I announce myself to you,
This gentle call is for you my love, for you.

Do not be decoy'd elsewhere,
That is the whistle of the wind, it is not my voice,
That is the fluttering, the fluttering of the spray,
Those are the shadows of leaves.

O darkness! O in vain!
O I am very sick and sorrowful.   120

O brown halo in the sky near the moon, drooping upon the sea!
O troubled reflection in the sea!
O throat! O throbbing heart!
And I singing uselessly, uselessly all the night.

O past! O happy life! O songs of joy!
In the air, in the woods, over fields,
Loved! loved! loved! loved! loved!
But my mate no more, no more with me!
We two together no more.

The aria sinking,   130
All else continuing, the stars shining.
The winds blowing, the notes of the bird continuous echoing.
With angry moans the fierce old mother incessantly moan-
    ing,
On the sands of Paumanok's shore gray and rustling,
The yellow half-moon enlarged, sagging down, drooping, the
    face of the sea almost touching,
The boy ecstatic, with his bare feet the waves, with his hair
    the atmosphere dallying,
The love in the heart long pent, now loose, now at last tumul-
    tuously bursting,
The aria's meaning, the ears, the soul, swiftly depositing,
The strange tears down the cheeks coursing,
The colloquy there, the trio, each uttering,   140
The undertone, the savage old mother incessantly crying,

To the boy's soul's questions sullenly timing, some drown'd
    secret hissing.
To the outsetting bard.

Demon or bird! (said the boy's soul,)
Is it indeed toward your mate you sing? or is it really to me?
For I, that was a child, my tongue's use sleeping, now I have
    heard you,
Now in a moment I know what I am for, I awake,
And already a thousand singers, a thousand songs, clearer,
    louder and more sorrowful than yours,
A thousand warbling echoes have started to life within me,
    never to die.

O you singer solitary, singing by yourself, projecting me,   150
O solitary me listening, never more shall I cease perpetuating
    you,
Never more shall I escape, never more the reverberations,
Never more the cries of unsatisfied love be absent from me,
Never again leave me to be the peaceful child I was before
    what there in the night,
By the sea under the yellow and sagging moon,
The messenger there arous'd, the fire, the sweet hell within,
The unknown want, the destiny of me.

O give me the clew! (it lurks in the night here somewhere,)
O if I am to have so much, let me have more!

A word then, (for I will conquer it,)   160
A word final, superior to all,
Subtle, sent-up what is it? – I listen;
Are you whispering it, and have been all the time, you sea
    waves?
Is that it from your liquid rims and wet sands?
Whereto answering, the sea,
Delaying not, hurrying not,
Whisper'd me through the night, and very plainly before
    daybreak,
Lisp'd to me the low and delicious word death,
And again death, death, death, death,

Hissing melodious, neither like the bird nor like my arous'd
    child's heart,   170
But edging near as privately for me rustling at my feet,
Creeping thence steadily up to my ears and laving me softly
    all over,
Death, death, death, death, death.

Which I do not forget,
But fuse the song of my dusky demon and brother,
That he sang to me in the moonlight on Paumanok's gray
    beach,
With the thousand reponsive songs at random,
My own songs awaked from that hour,
And with them the key, the word up from the waves,
The word of the sweetest song and all songs,   180
That strong and delicious word which, creeping to my feet,
(Or like some old crone rocking the cradle, swathed in sweet
    garments, bending aside,)
The sea whisper'd me.

1859   1881

As I Ebb'd with the Ocean of Life

1

As I ebb'd with the ocean of life,
As I wended the shores I know,
As I walk'd where the ripples continually wash you Pauma-
    nok,
Where they rustle up hoarse and sibilant,
Where the fierce old mother endlessly cries for her castaways,
I musing late in the autumn day, gazing off southward,
Held by this electric self out of the pride of which I utter
    poems,
Was seiz'd by the spirit that trails in the lines underfoot,

The rim, the sediment that stands for all the water and all the
    land of the globe.

Fascinated, my eyes reverting from the south, dropt, to follow
    those slender windrows,   10
Chaff, straw, splinters of wood, weeds, and the sea-gluten,
Scum, scales from shining rocks, leaves of salt-lettuce, left by
    the tide,
Miles walking, the sound of breaking waves the other side of
    me,
Paumanok there and then as I thought the old thought of
    likenesses,
These you presented to me you fish-shaped island,
As I wended the shores I know,
As I walk'd with that electric self-seeking types.

2

As I wend to the shores I know not,
As I list to the dirge, the voices of men and women wreck'd
As I inhale the impalpable breezes that set in upon me,   20
As the ocean so mysterious rolls toward me closer and closer,
I too but signify at the utmost a little wash'd-up drift,
A few sands and dead leaves to gather,
Gather, and merge myself as part of the sands and drift.

O baffled, balk'd, bent to the very earth,
Oppress'd with myself that I have dared to open my mouth,
Aware now that amid all that blab whose echoes recoil upon
    me I have not once had the least idea who or what I am,
But that before all my arrogant poems the real Me stands yet
    untouch'd, untold, altogether unreach'd,
Withdrawn far, mocking me with mock-congratulatory signs
    and bows,
With peals of distant ironical laughter at every word I have
    written,   30
Pointing in silence to these songs, and then to the sand
    beneath.
I perceive I have not really understood any thing, not a single
    object, and that no man ever can,

Nature here in sight of the sea taking advantage of me to dart
    upon me and sting me,
Because I have dared to open my mouth to sing at all.

3

You oceans both, I close with you,
We murmur alike reproachfully rolling sands and drift,
    knowing not why,
These little shreds indeed standing for you and me and all.
You friable shore with trails of debris,
You fish-shaped island, I take what is underfoot,
What is yours is mine my father.   40

I too Paumanok,
I too have bubbled up, floated the measureless float, and been
    wash'd on your shores,
I too am but a trail of drift and debris,
I too leave little wrecks upon you, you fish-shaped island.

I throw myself upon your breast my father,
I cling to you so that you cannot unloose me,
I hold you so firm till you answer me something.

Kiss me my father,
Touch me with your lips as I touch those I love,
Breathe to me while I hold you close the secret of the mur-
    muring I envy.   50

4

Ebb, ocean of life, (the flow will return,)
Cease not your moaning you fierce old mother,
Endlessly cry for your castaways, but fear not, deny not me,
Rustle not up so hoarse and angry against my feet as I touch
    you or gather from you.

I mean tenderly by you and all,
I gather for myself and for this phantom looking down where
    we lead, and following me and mine.

Me and mine, loose windrows, little corpses,

Froth, snowy white, and bubbles,
(See, from my dead lips the ooze exuding at last,
See, the prismatic colors glistening and rolling,)   60
Tufts of straw, sands, fragments,
Buoy'd hither from many moods, one contradicting another,
From the storm, the long calm, the darkness, the swell,
Musing, pondering, a breath, a briny tear, a dab of liquid or
    soil,
Up just as much out of fathomless workings fermented and
    thrown,
A limp blossom or two, torn, just as much over waves
    floating, drifted at random,
Just as much for us that sobbing dirge of Nature,
Just as much whence we come that blare of the cloud-
    trumpets,
We, capricious, brought hither we know not whence, spread
    out before you,
You up there walking or sitting,
Whoever you are, we too lie in drifts at your feet.

1860   1881

I Sing the Body Electric

1

I sing the body electric,
The armies of those I love engirth me and I engirth them,
They will not let me off till I go with them, respond to them,
And discorrupt them, and charge them full with the charge of
    the soul.

Was it doubted that those who corrupt their own bodies
    conceal themselves?
And if those who defile the living are as bad as they who defile
    the dead?
And if the body does not do fully as much as the soul?
And if the body were not the soul, what is the soul?

2

The love of the body of man or woman balks account, the
    body itself balks account,
That of the male is perfect, and that of the female is perfect.   10

The expression of the face balks account,
But the expression of a well-made man appears not only in his
    face,
It is in his limbs and joints also, it is curiously in the joints of
    his hips and wrists,
It is in his walk, the carriage of his neck, the flex of his waist
    and knees, dress does not hide him,
The strong sweet quality he has strikes through the cotton
    and broadcloth,
To see him pass conveys as much as the best poem, perhaps
    more,
You linger to see his back, and the back of his neck and
    shoulder-side.

The sprawl and fulness of babes, the bosoms and heads of
    women, the folds of their dress, their style as we pass in the
    street, the contour of their shape downwards,
The swimmer naked in the swimming-bath, seen as he swims
    through the transparent green-shine, or lies with his face
    up and rolls silently to and fro in the heave of the water,
The bending forward and backward of rowers in row-boats,
    the horseman in his saddle,   20
Girls, mothers, house-keepers, in all their performances,
The group of laborers seated at noon-time with their open
    dinner-kettles, and their wives waiting,
The female soothing a child, the farmer's daughter in the
    garden or cow-yard,
The young fellow hoeing corn, the sleigh-driver driving his
    six horses through the crowd,
The wrestle of wrestlers, two apprentice-boys, quite grown,
    lusty, good-natured, native-born, out on the vacant lot at
    sundown after work,
The coats and caps thrown down, the embrace of love and
    resistance,

The upper-hold and under-hold, the hair rumpled over and
    blinding the eyes;
The march of firemen in their own costumes, the play of
    masculine muscle through clean-setting trowsers and
    waist-straps,
The slow return from the fire, the pause when the bell strikes
    suddenly again, and the listening on the alert,
The natural, perfect, varied attitudes, the bent head, the
    curv'd neck and the counting;   30
Such-like I love – I loosen myself, pass freely, am at the
    mother's breast with the little child,
Swim with the swimmers, wrestle with wrestlers, march in
    line with the firemen, and pause, listen, count.

3

I knew a man, a common farmer, the father of five sons,
And in them the fathers of sons, and in them the fathers of
    sons.

This man was of wonderful vigor, calmness, beauty of person,
The shape of his head, the pale yellow and white of his hair
    and beard, the immeasurable meaning of his black eyes,
    the richness and breadth of his manners,
These I used to go and visit him to see, he was wise also,
He was six feet tall, he was over eighty years old, his sons were
    massive, clean, bearded, tan-faced, handsome,
They and his daughters loved him, all who saw him loved
    him,
They did not love him by allowance, they loved him with
    personal love,   40
He drank water only, the blood show'd like scarlet through
    the clear-brown skin of his face,
He was a frequent gunner and fisher, he sail'd his boat
    himself, he had a fine one presented to him by a ship-
    joiner, he had fowling-pieces presented to him by men that
    loved him,
When he went with his five sons and many grand-sons to
    hunt or fish, you would pick him out as the most beautiful
    and vigorous of the gang,
You would wish long and long to be with him, you would

wish to sit by him in the boat that you and he might touch each other.

4

I have perceiv'd that to be with those I like is enough,
To stop in company with the rest at evening is enough,
To be surrounded by beautiful, curious, breathing, laughing flesh is enough,
To pass among them or touch any one, or rest my arm ever so lightly round his or her neck for a moment, what is this then?
I do not ask any more delight, I swim in it as in a sea.

There is something in staying close to men and women and looking on them, and in the contact and odor of them, that pleases the soul well,   50
All things please the soul, but these please the soul well.

5

This is the female form,
A divine nimbus exhales from it from head to foot,
It attracts with fierce undeniable attraction,
I am drawn by its breath as if I were no more than a helpless vapor, all falls aside but myself and it,
Books, art, religion, time, the visible and solid earth, and what was expected of heaven or fear'd of hell, are now consumed.
Mad filaments, ungovernable shoots play out of it, the response likewise ungovernable,
Hair, bosom, hips, bend of legs, negligent falling hands all diffused, mine too diffused,
Ebb stung by the flow and flow stung by the ebb, love-flesh swelling and deliciously aching,
Limitless limpid jets of love hot and enormous, quivering jelly of love, white-blow and delirious juice,   60
Bridegroom night of love working surely and softly into the prostrate dawn,
Undulating into the willing and yielding day,
Lost in the cleave of the clasping and sweet-flesh'd day.

*

This the nucleus – after the child is born of woman, man is
     born of woman,
This the bath of birth, this the merge of small and large, and
     the outlet again.

Be not ashamed women, your privilege encloses the rest, and
     is the exit of the rest,
You are the gates of the body, and you are the gates of the
     soul.

The female contains all qualities and tempers them,
She is in her place and moves with perfect balance,
She is all things duly veil'd, she is both passive and active,   70
She is to conceive daughters as well as sons, and sons as well
     as daughters.

As I see my soul reflected in Nature,
As I see through a mist, One with inexpressible completeness,
     sanity, beauty,
See the bent head and arms folded over the breast, the Female
     I see.

6

The male is not less the soul nor more, he too is in his place,
He too is all qualities, he is action and power,
The flush of the known universe is in him,
Scorn becomes him well, and appetite and defiance become
     him well,
The wildest largest passions, bliss that is utmost, sorrow that
     is utmost become him well, pride is for him,
The full-spread pride of man is calming and excellent to the
     soul,   80
Knowledge becomes him, he likes it always, he brings every
     thing to the test of himself,
Whatever the survey, whatever the sea and the sail he strikes
     soundings as last only here,
(Where else does he strike soundings except here?)
The man's body is sacred and the woman's body is sacred,
No matter who it is, it is sacred – is it the meanest one in the
     laborer's gang?

Is it one of the dull-faced immigrants just landed on the
    wharf?
Each belongs here or anywhere just as much as the well-off,
    just as much as you,
Each has his or her place in the procession.

(All is a procession,
The universe is a procession with measured and perfect
    motion.)   90

Do you know so much yourself that you call the meanest
    ignorant?
Do you suppose you have a right to a good sight, and he or she
    has no right to a sight?
Do you think matter has cohered together from its diffuse
    float, and the soil is on the surface, and water runs and
    vegetation sprouts,
For you only, and not for him and her?

                        7

A man's body at auction,
(For before the war I often go to the slave-mart and watch the
    sale,)
I help the auctioneer, the sloven does not half know his
    business.

Gentlemen look on this wonder,
Whatever the bids of the bidders they cannot be high enough
    for it,
For it the globe lay preparing quintillions of years without one
    animal or plant,   100
For it the revolving cycles truly and steadily roll'd.

In this head the all-baffling brain,
In it and below it the makings of heroes.

Examine these limbs, red, black, or white, they are cunning in
    tendon and nerve,
They shall be stript that you may see them.
Exquisite senses, life-lit eyes, pluck, volition,

Flakes of breast-muscle, pliant backbone and neck, flesh not
    flabby, good-sized arms and legs,
And wonders within there yet.

Within there runs blood,
The same old blood! the same red-running blood!   110
There swells and jets a heart, there all passions, desires,
    reachings, aspirations,
(Do you think they are not there because they are not
    express'd in parlors and lecture-rooms?)

This is not only one man, this the father of those who shall be
    fathers in their turns,
In him the start of populous states and rich republics,
Of him countless immortal lives with countless embodiments
    and enjoyments.

How do you know who shall come from the offspring of his
    offspring through the centuries?
(Who might you find you have come from yourself, if you
    could trace back through the centuries?)

8

A woman's body at auction,
She too is not only herself, she is the teeming mother of
    mothers,
She is the bearer of them that shall grow and be mates to the
    mothers.   120

Have you ever loved the body of a woman?
Have you ever loved the body of a man?
Do you not see that these are exactly the same to all in all
    nations and times all over the earth?
If any thing is sacred the human body is sacred,
And the glory and sweat of a man is the token of manhood
    untainted,
And in man or woman a clean, strong, firm-fibred body, is
    more beautiful than the most beautiful face.
Have you seen the fool that corrupted his own live body? or
    the fool that corrupted her own live body?

For they do not conceal themselves, and cannot conceal
    themselves.

9

O my body! I dare not desert the likes of you in other men and
    women, nor the likes of the parts of you,

I believe the likes of you are to stand or fall with the likes of the
    soul (and that they are the soul,)   130

I believe the likes of you shall stand or fall with my poems, and
    that they are my poems,

Man's, woman's, child's, youth's, wife's, husband's, moth-
    er's, father's, young man's, young woman's poems,

Head, neck, hair, ears, drop and tympan of the ears,

Eyes, eye-fringes, iris of the eye, eyebrows, and the waking or
    sleeping of the lids,

Mouth, tongue, lips, teeth, roof of the mouth, jaws, and the
    jaw-hinges,

Nose, nostrils of the nose, and the partition,

Cheeks, temples, forehead, chin, throat, back of the neck,
    neck-slue,

Strong shoulders, manly beard, scapula, hind-shoulders, and
    the ample side-round of the chest,

Upper-arm, armpit, elbow-socket, lower-arm, arm-sinews,
    arm-bones,

Wrist and wrist-joints, hand, palm, knuckles, thumb, fore-
    finger, finger-joints, finger-nails,   140

Broad breast-front, curling hair of the breast, breast-bone,
    breast-side,

Ribs, belly, backbone, joints of the backbone,

Hips, hip-sockets, hip-strength, inward and outward round,
    man-balls, man-root,

Strong set of thighs, well carrying the trunk above,

Leg-fibres, knee, knee-pan, upper-leg, under-leg,

Ankles, instep, foot-ball, toes, toe-joints, the heel;

All attitudes, all the shapeliness, all the belongings of my or
    your body or of any one's body, male or female,

The lung-sponges, the stomach-sac, the bowels sweet and
    clean,

The brain in its folds inside the skull-frame,

Sympathies, heart-valves, palate-valves, sexuality, maternity,   150

Womanhood and all that is a woman, and the man that
    comes from woman,

The womb, the teats, nipples, breast-milk, tears, laughter,
    weeping, love-looks, love-perturbations and risings,

The voice, articulation, language, whispering, shouting
    aloud,

Food, drink, pulse, digestion, sweat, sleep, walking, swim-
    ming,

Poise on the hips, leaping, reclining, embracing, arm-curving
    and tightening,

The continual changes of the flex of the mouth, and around
    the eyes,

The skin, the sunburnt shade, freckles, hair,

The curious sympathy one feels when feeling with the hand
    the naked meat of the body,

The circling rivers the breath, and breathing it in and out,

The beauty of the waist, and thence of the hips, and thence
    downward toward the knees,   160

The thin red jellies within you or within me, the bones and
    the marrow in the bones,

The exquisite realization of health;

O I say these are not the parts and poems of the body only, but
    of the soul,

O I say now these are the soul!

1855   1881

Spontaneous Me

Spontaneous me, Nature,

The loving day, the mounting sun, the friend I am happy
    with,

The arm of my friend hanging idly over my shoulder,

The hillside whiten'd with blossoms of the mountain ash,

The same late in autumn, the hues of red, yellow, drab,
    purple, and light and dark green,

The rich coverlet of the grass, animals and birds, the private
    untrimm'd bank, the primitive apples, the pebble-stones,
Beautiful dripping fragments, the negligent list of one after
    another as I happen to call them to me or think of them,
The real poems, (what we call poems being merely pictures,)
The poems of the privacy of the night, and of men like me,
This poem drooping shy and unseen that I always carry, and
    that all men carry.   10
(Know once for all, avow'd on purpose, wherever are men
    like me, are our lusty lurking masculine poems,)
Love-thoughts, love-juice, love-odor, love-yielding, love-
    climbers, and the climbing sap,
Arms and hands of love, lips of love, phallic thumb of love,
    breasts of love, bellies press'd and glued together with love,
Earth of chaste love, life that is only life after love,
The body of my love, the body of the woman I love, the body
    of the man, the body of the earth,
Soft forenoon airs that blow from the south-west,
The hairy wild-bee that murmurs and hankers up and down,
    that gripes the full-grown lady-flower, curves upon her
    with amorous firm legs, takes his will of her, and holds
    himself tremulous and tight till he is satisfied;
The wet of woods through the early hours,
Two sleepers at night lying close together as they sleep, one
    with an arm slanting down across and below the waist of
    the other,
The smell of apples, aromas from crush'd sage-plant, mint,
    birch-bark,   20
The boy's longings, the glow and pressure as he confides to
    me what he was dreaming,
The dead leaf whirling its spiral whirl and falling still and
    content to the ground,
The no-form'd stings that sights, people, objects, sting me
    with,
The hubb'd sting of myself, stinging me as much as it ever can
    any one,
The sensitive, orbic, underlapp'd brothers, that only privil-
    leged feelers may be intimate where they are,
The curious roamer the hand roaming all over the body, the
    bashful withdrawing of flesh where the fingers soothingly
    pause and edge themselves,

The limpid liquid within the young man,
The vex'd corrosion so pensive and so painful,
The torment, the irritable tide that will not be at rest,
The like of the same I feel, the like of the same in others,   30
The young man that flushes and flushes, and the young
    woman that flushes and flushes,
The young man that wakes deep at night, the hot hand
    seeking to repress what would master him,
The mystic amorous night, the strange half-welcome pangs,
    visions, sweats,
The pulse pounding through palms and trembling encircling
    fingers, the young man all color'd, red, ashamed, angry;
The souse upon me of my lover the sea, as I lie willing and
    naked,
The merriment of the twin babes that crawl over the grass in
    the sun, the mother never turning her vigilant eyes from
    them,
The walnut-trunk, the walnut-husks, and the ripening or
    ripen'd long-round walnuts,
The continence of vegetables, birds, animals,
The consequent meanness of me should I skulk or find myself
    indecent, while birds and animals never once skulk or find
    themselves indecent,
The great chastity of paternity, to match the great chastity of
    maternity,   40
The oath of procreation I have sworn, my Adamic and fresh
    daughters,
The greed that eats me day and night with hungry gnaw, till I
    saturate what shall produce boys to fill my place when I
    am through,
The wholesome relief, repose, content,
And this bunch pluck'd at random from myself,
It has done its work – I toss it carelessly to fall where it may.

    1856   1867

As Adam Early in the Morning

As Adam early in the morning,
Walking forth from the bower refresh'd with sleep,
Behold me where I pass, hear my voice, approach,
Touch me, touch the palm of your hand to my body as I pass,
Be not afraid of my body.

1860   1867

In Paths Untrodden

In paths untrodden,
In the growths by margins of pond-waters,
Escaped from the life that exhibits itself,
From all the standards hitherto publish'd, from the pleasures,
    profits, conformities,
Which too long I was offering to feed my soul,
Clear to me now standards not yet publish'd, clear to me that
    my soul,
That the soul of the man I speak for rejoices in comrades,
Here by myself away from the clank of the world,
Tallying and talk'd to here by tongues aromatic,
No longer abash'd (for in this secluded spot I can respond as
    I would not dare elsewhere,)   10
Strong upon me the life that does not exhibit itself, yet
    contains all the rest,
Resolv'd to sing no songs to-day but those of manly attach-
    ment,
Projecting them along that substantial life,
Bequeathing hence types of athletic love,
Afternoon this delicious Ninth-month in my forty-first year,
I proceed for all who are or have been young men,
To tell the secret of my nights and days,
To celebrate the need of comrades.

1860   1867

We Two, How Long We Were Fool'd

We two, how long we were fool'd,
Now transmuted, we swiftly escape as Nature escapes,
We are Nature, long have we been absent, but now we
    return,
We become plants, trunks, foliage, roots, bark,
We are bedded in the ground, we are rocks,
We are oaks, we grow in the openings side by side,
We browse, we are two among the wild herds spontaneous as
    any,
We are two fishes swimming in the sea together,
We are what locust blossoms are, we drop scent around lanes
    mornings and evenings,
We are also the coarse smut of beasts, vegetables, minerals,   10
We are two predatory hawks, we soar above and look down,
We are two resplendent suns, we it is who balance ourselves
    orbic and stellar, we are as two comets,
We prowl fang'd and four-footed in the woods, we spring on
    prey,
We are two clouds forenoons and afternoons driving over-
    head,
We are seas mingling, we are two of those cheerful waves
    rolling over each other and interwetting each other,
We are what the atmosphere is, transparent, receptive,
    pervious, impervious,
We are snow, rain, cold, darkness, we are each product and
    influence of the globe,
We have circled and circled till we have arrived home again,
    we two,
We have voided all but freedom and all but our own joy.

1860   1881

Native Moments

Native moments – when you come upon me – ah you are here
    now,
Give me now libidinous joys only,
Give me the drench of my passions, give me life coarse and
    rank,
To-day I go consort with Nature's darlings, to-night too,
I am for those who believe in loose delights, I share the mid-
    night orgies of young men,
I dance with the dancers and drink with the drinkers,
The echoes ring with our indecent calls, I pick out some low
    person for my dearest friend,
He shall be lawless, rude, illiterate, he shall be one con-
    demned by others for deeds done,
I will play a part no longer, why should I exile myself from my
    companions?
O you shunn'd persons, I at least do not shun you,   10
I come forthwith in your midst, I will be your poet,
I will be more to you than to any of the rest.

1860   1881

These I Singing in Spring

These I singing in spring collect for lovers,
(For who but I should understand lovers and all their sorrow
    and joy?
And who but I should be the poet of comrades?)
Collecting I traverse the garden the world, but soon I pass the
    gates,
Now along the pond-side, now wading in a little, fearing not
    the wet,
Now by the post-and-rail fences where the old stones thrown
    there, pick'd from the fields, have accumulated,

(Wild-flowers and vines and weeds come up through the
     stones and partly cover them, beyond these I pass,)
For, far in the forest, or sauntering later in summer, before I
     think where I go,
Solitary, smelling the earthy smell, stopping now and then in
     the silence,
Alone I had thought, yet soon a troop gathers around me,   10
Some walk by my side and some behind, and some embrace
     my arms or neck,
They the spirits of dear friends dead or alive, thicker they
     come, a great crowd, and I in the middle,
Collecting, dispensing, singing, there I wander with them,
Plucking something for tokens, tossing toward whoever is
     near me,
Here, lilac, with a branch of pine,
Here, out of my pocket, some moss which I pull'd off a live-oak
     in Florida as it hung trailing down,
Here, some pinks and laurel leaves, and a handful of sage,
And here what I now draw from the water, wading in the
     pond-side,
(O here I last saw him that tenderly loves me, and returns
     again never to separate from me,
And this, O this shall henceforth be the token of comrades,
     this calamus-root shall,   20
Interchange it youths with each other! let none render it
     back!)
And twigs of maple and a bunch of wild orange and chestnut,
And stems of currants and plum-blows, and the aromatic
     cedar,
These I compass'd around by a thick cloud of spirits,
Wandering, point to or touch as I pass, or throw them loosely
     from me,
Indicating to each one what he shall have, giving something
     to each;
But what I drew from the water by the pond-side, that I
     reserve,
I will give it, but only to them that love as I myself am capable
     of loving.

     1860   1867

A Glimpse

A glimpse through an interstice caught,
Of a crowd of workmen and drivers in a bar-room around the
    stove late of a winter night, and I unremark'd seated in a
    corner,
Of a youth who loves me and whom I love, silently ap-
        proaching and seating himself near, that he may hold
    me by the hand,
A long while amid the noises of coming and going, of drinking
    and oath and smutty jest,
There we two, content, happy in being together, speaking
    little, perhaps not a word.

1860   1867

I Saw in Louisiana a Live-Oak Growing

I saw in Louisiana a live-oak growing,
All alone stood it and the moss hung down from the branches,
Without any companion it grew there uttering joyous leaves
    of dark green,
And its look, rude, unbending, lusty, made me think of
    myself,
But I wonder'd how it could utter joyous leaves standing
    alone there without its friend near, for I knew I could not,
And I broke off a twig with a certain number of leaves upon it,
    and twined around it a little moss,
And brought it away, and I have placed it in sight, in my
    room,
It is not needed to remind me as of my own dear friends,
(For I believe lately I think of little else than of them,)
Yet it remains to me a curious token, it makes me think of
    manly love;   10
For all that, and though the live-oak glistens there in
    Louisiana solitary in a wide flat space,

Uttering joyous leaves all its life without a friend a lover near,
I know very well I could not.

1860   1867

Scented Herbage of My Breast

Scented herbage of my breast,
Leaves from you I glean, I write, to be perused best
     afterwards,
Tomb-leaves, body-leaves growing up above me above death,
Perennial roots, tall leaves, O the winter shall not freeze you
     delicate leaves,
Every year shall you bloom again, out from where you retired
     you shall emerge again;
O I do not know whether many passing by will discover you
     or inhale your faint odor, but I believe a few will;
O slender leaves! O blossoms of my blood! I permit you to tell
     in your own way of the heart that is under you,
O I do not know what you mean there underneath your-
     selves, you are not happiness,
You are often more bitter than I can bear, you burn and sting
     me,
Yet you are beautiful to me you faint tinged roots, you make
     me think of death,   10
Death is beautiful from you, (what indeed is finally beautiful
     except death and love?)
O I think it is not for life I am chanting here my chant of
     lovers, I think it must be for death,
For how calm, how solemn it grows to ascend to the
     atmosphere of lovers,
Death or life I am then indifferent, my soul declines to prefer,
(I am not sure but the high soul of lovers welcomes death
     most,)
Indeed O death, I think now these leaves mean precisely the
     same as you mean,

Grow up taller sweet leaves that I may see! grow up out of my
 breast!
Spring away from the conceal'd heart there!
Do not fold yourself so in your pink-tinged roots timid leaves!
Do not remain down there so ashamed, herbage of my breast!
Come I am determin'd to unbare this broad breast of mine, I
 have long enough stifled and choked;   20
Emblematic and capricious blades I leave you, now you serve
 me not,
I will say what I have to say by itself,
I will sound myself and comrades only, I will never again
 utter a call only their call,
I will raise with it immortal reverberations through the
 States,
I will give an example to lovers to take permanent shape and
 will through the States,
Through me shall the words be said to make death exhilar-
 ating,
Give me your tone therefore O death, that I may accord with
 it,
Give me yourself, for I see that you belong to me now above
 all, and are folded inseparably together, you love and
 death are,
Nor will I allow you to balk me any more with what I was
 calling life,
For now it is convey'd to me that you are the purports
 essential,   30
That you hide in these shifting forms of life, for reasons, and
 that they are mainly for you,
That you beyond them come forth to remain, the real reality,
That behind the mask of materials you patiently wait, no
 matter how long,
That you will one day perhaps take control of all,
That you will perhaps dissipate this entire show of appear-
 ance,
That may-be you are what it is all for, but it does not last so
 very long,
But you will last very long.

1860   1867

Of the Terrible Doubt of Appearances

Of the terrible doubt of appearances,
Of the uncertainty after all, that we may be deluded,
That may-be reliance and hope are but speculations after all,
That may-be identity beyond the grave is a beautiful fable
    only,
May-be the things I perceive, the animals, plants, men, hills,
    shining and flowing waters,
The skies of day and night, colors, densities, forms, may-be
    these are (as doubtless they are) only apparitions, and the
    real something has yet to be known,
(How often they dart out of themselves as if to confound me
    and mock me!
How often I think neither I know, nor any man knows, aught
    of them,)
May-be seeming to me what they are (as doubtless they
    indeed but seem) as from my present point of view, and
    might prove (as of course they would) nought of what they
    appear, or nought anyhow, from entirely changed points
    of view;
To me these and the like of these are curiously answer'd by
    my lovers, my dear friends,   10
When he whom I love travels with me or sits a long while
    holding me by the hand,
When the subtle air, the impalpable, the sense that words and
    reason hold not, surround us and pervade us,
Then I am charged with untold and untellable wisdom, I am
    silent, I require nothing further,
I cannot answer the question of appearances or that of iden-
    tity beyond the grave,
But I walk or sit indifferent, I am satisfied,
He ahold of my hand has completely satisfied me.

1860   1867

A March in the Ranks Hard-Prest, and the Road Unknown

A march in the ranks hard-prest, and the road unknown,
A route through a heavy wood with muffled steps in the
     darkness,
Our army foil'd with loss severe, and the sullen remnant
     retreating,
Till after midnight glimmer upon us the lights of a dim-lighted
     building,
We come to an open space in the woods, and halt by the dim-
     lighted building,
'Tis a large old church at the crossing roads, now an
     impromptu hospital,
Entering but for a minute I see a sight beyond all the pictures
     and poems ever made,
Shadows of deepest, deepest black, just lit by moving candles
     and lamps,
And by one great pitchy torch stationary with wild red flame
     and clouds of smoke,
By these, crowds, groups of forms vaguely I see on the floor,
     some in the pews laid down,   10
At my feet more distinctly a soldier, a mere lad, in danger of
     bleeding to death, (he is shot in the abdomen,)
I staunch the blood temporarily, (the youngster's face is white
     as a lily,)
Then before I depart I sweep my eyes o'er the scene fain to
     absorb it all,
Faces, varieties, postures beyond description, most in obscur-
     ity, some of them dead,
Surgeons operating, attendants holding lights, the smell of
     ether, the odor of blood,
The crowd, O the crowd of the bloody forms, the yard outside
     also fill'd,
Some on the bare ground, some on planks or stretchers, some
     in the death-spasm sweating,
An occasional scream or cry, the doctor's shouted orders or
     calls,

The glisten of the little steel instruments catching the glint of
    the torches,
These I resume as I chant, I see again the forms, I smell the
    odor,   20
Then hear outside the orders given, *Fall in, my men, fall in*;
But first I bend to the dying lad, his eyes open, a half-smile
    gives he me,
Then the eyes close, calmly close, and I speed forth to the
    darkness,
Resuming, marching, ever in darkness marching, on in the
    ranks,
The unknown road still marching.

1865   1867

The Wound-Dresser

1

An old man bending I come among new faces,
Years looking backward resuming in answer to children,
Come tell us old man, as from young men and maidens that
    love me,
(Arous'd and angry, I'd thought to beat the alarum, and urge
    relentless war,
But soon my fingers fail'd me, my face droop'd and I resign'd
    myself,
To sit by the wounded and soothe them, or silently watch the
    dead;)
Years hence of these scenes, of these furious passions, these
    chances,
Of unsurpass'd heroes, (was one side so brave? the other was
    equally brave;)
Now be witness again, paint the mightiest armies of earth,
Of those armies so rapid so wondrous what saw you to tell us?   10
What stays with you latest and deepest? of curious panics,
Of hard-fought engagements or sieges tremendous what
    deepest remains?

2

O maidens and young men I love and that love me,

What you ask of my days those the strangest and sudden your
talking recalls,

Soldier alert I arrive after a long march cover'd with sweat
and dust,

In the nick of time I come, plunge in the fight, loudly shout in
the rush of successful charge,

Enter the captur'd works – yet lo, like a swift running river
they fade,

Pass and are gone they fade – I dwell not on soldiers' perils or
soldiers' joys,

(Both I remember well – many of the hardships, few the joys,
yet I was content.)

But in silence, in dreams' projections,   20

While the world of gain and appearance and mirth goes on,

So soon what is over forgotten, and waves wash the imprints
off the sand,

With hinged knees returning I enter the doors, (while for you
up there,

Whoever you are, follow without noise and be of strong
heart.)

Bearing the bandages, water and sponge,

Straight and swift to my wounded I go,

Where they lie on the ground after the battle brought in,

Where their priceless blood reddens the grass the ground,

Or to the rows of the hospital tent, or under the roof'd
hospital,

To the long rows of cots up and down each side I return,   30

To each and all one after another I draw near, not one do I
miss,

An attendant follows holding a tray, he carries a refuse pail,

Soon to be fill'd with clotted rags and blood, emptied, and
fill'd again.

I onward go, I stop,

With hinged knees and steady hand to dress wounds,

I am firm with each, the pangs are sharp yet unavoidable,

One turns to me his appealing eyes – poor boy! I never knew
    you,
Yet I think I could not refuse this moment to die for you, if that
    would save you.

3

On, on I go, (open doors of time! open hospital doors!)
The crush'd head I dress, (poor crazed hand tear not the
    bandage away,)   40
The neck of the cavalry-man with the bullet through and
    through I examine,
Hard the breathing rattles, quite glazed already the eye, yet
    life struggles hard,
(Come sweet death! be persuaded O beautiful death!
In mercy come quickly.)

From the stump of the arm, the amputated hand,
I undo the clotted lint, remove the slough, wash off the matter
    and blood,
Back on his pillow the soldier bends with curv'd neck and side
    falling head,
His eyes are closed, his face is pale, he dares not look on the
    bloody stump,
And has not yet look'd on it.

I dress a wound in the side, deep, deep,   50
But a day or two more, for see the frame all wasted and
    sinking,
And the yellow-blue countenance see.

I dress the perforated shoulder, the foot with the bullet-
    wound,
Cleanse the one with a gnawing and putrid gangrene, so
    sickening, so offensive,
While the attendant stands behind aside me holding the tray
    and pail.

I am faithful, I do not give out,
The fractur'd thigh, the knee, the wound in the abdomen,

These and more I dress with impassive hand, (yet deep in my
    breast a fire, a burning flame.)

4

Thus in silence in dreams' projections,
Returning, resuming, I thread my way through the hospitals,   60
The hurt and wounded I pacify with soothing hand,
I sit by the restless all the dark night, some are so young,
Some suffer so much, I recall the experience sweet and sad,
(Many a soldier's loving arms about this neck have cross'd
    and rested,
Many a soldier's kiss dwells on these bearded lips.)

1865   1881

Reconciliation

Word over all, beautiful as the sky,
Beautiful that war and all its deeds of carnage must in time be
    utterly lost,
That the hands of the sisters Death and Night incessantly
    softly wash again, and ever again, this soil'd world;
For my enemy is dead, a man divine as myself is dead,
I look where he lies white-faced and still in the coffin – I draw
    near,
Bend down and touch lightly with my lips the white face in
    the coffin.

1865–6   1881

When Lilacs Last in the Dooryard Bloom'd

1

When lilacs last in the dooryard bloom'd,
And the great star early droop'd in the western sky in the
    night,
I mourn'd, and yet shall mourn with ever-returning spring.

Ever-returning spring, trinity sure to me you bring,
Lilac blooming perennial and drooping star in the west,
And thought of him I love.

2

O powerful western fallen star!
O shades of night – O moody, tearful night!
O great star disappear'd – O the black murk that hides the
    star!
O cruel hands that hold me powerless – O helpless soul of me!   10
O harsh surrounding cloud that will not free my soul.

3

In the dooryard fronting an old farm-house near the white-
    wash'd palings,
Stands the lilac-bush tall-growing with heart-shaped leaves
    of rich green,
With many a pointed blossom rising delicate, with the
    perfume strong I love,
With every leaf a miracle – and from this bush in the door-
    yard,
With delicate-color'd blossoms and heart-shaped leaves of
    rich green,
A sprig with its flower I break.

4

In the swamp in secluded recesses,
A shy and hidden bird is warbling a song.

Solitary the thrush,   20
The hermit withdrawn to himself, avoiding the settlements,

Sings by himself a song.

Song of the bleeding throat,
Death's outlet song of life, (for well dear brother I knew,
If thou wast not granted to sing thou would'st surely die.)

5

Over the breast of the spring, the land, amid cities,
Amid lanes and through old woods, where lately the violets
    peep'd from the ground, spotting the gray debris,
Amid the grass in the fields each side of the lanes, passing the
    endless grass,
Passing the yellow-spear'd wheat, every grain from its shroud
    in the dark-brown fields uprisen,
Passing the apple-tree blows of white and pink in the
    orchards,   30
Carrying a corpse to where it shall rest in the grave,
Night and day journeys a coffin.

6

Coffin that passes through lanes and streets,
Through day and night with the great cloud darkening the
    land,
With the pomp of the inloop'd flags with the cities draped in
    black,
With the show of the States themselves as of crape-veil'd
    women standing,
With processions long and winding and the flambeaus of the
    night,
With the countless torches lit, with the silent sea of faces and
    the unbared heads,
With the waiting depot, the arriving coffin, and the somber
    faces,
With dirges through the night, with the thousand voices
    rising strong and solemn,   40
With all the mournful voices of the dirges pour'd around the
    coffin,
The dim-lit churches and the shuddering organs – where
    amid these you journey,
With the tolling tolling bells' perpetual clang,

Here, coffin that slowly passes,
I give you my sprig of lilac.

7

(Nor for you, for one alone,
Blossoms and branches green to coffins all I bring,
For fresh as the morning, thus would I chant a song for you
        O sane and sacred death.

All over bouquets of roses,
O death, I cover you over with roses and early lilies,   50
But mostly and now the lilac that blooms the first,
Copious I break, I break the sprigs from the bushes,
With loaded arms I come, pouring for you,
For you and the coffins all of you O death.)

8

O western orb sailing the heaven,
Now I know what you must have meant as a month since I
    walk'd,
As I walk'd in silence the transparent shadowy night,
As I saw you had something to tell as you bent to me night
    after night,
As you droop'd from the sky low down as if to my side, (while
    the other stars all look'd on,)
As we wander'd together the solemn night, (for something I
    know not what kept me from sleep,)   60
As the night advanced, and I saw on the rim of the west how
    full you were of woe,
As I stood on the rising ground in the breeze in the cool
    transparent night,
As I watch'd where you pass'd and was lost in the nether-
    ward black of the night,
As my soul in its trouble dissatisfied sank, as where you sad
    orb,
Concluded, dropt in the night, and was gone.

9

Sing on there in the swamp,
O singer bashful and tender, I hear your notes, I hear your

call,
I hear, I come presently, I understand you,
But a moment I linger, for the lustrous star has detain'd me,
The star my departing comrade holds and detains me.   70

10

O how shall I warble myself for the dead one there I loved?
And how shall I deck my song for the large sweet soul that
     has gone?
And what shall my perfume be for the grave of him I love?

Sea-winds blown from east and west,
Blown from the Eastern sea and blown from the Western sea,
     till there on the prairies meeting,
These and with these and the breath of my chant,
I'll perfume the grave of him I love.

11

O what shall I hang on the chamber walls?
And what shall the pictures be that I hang on the walls,
To adorn the burial-house of him I love?   80

Pictures of growing spring and farms and homes,
With the Fourth-month eve at sundown, and the gray smoke
     lucid and bright,
With floods of the yellow gold of the gorgeous, indolent,
     sinking sun, burning, expanding the air,
With the fresh sweet herbage under foot, and the pale green
     leaves of the trees prolific,
In the distance the flowing glaze, the breast of the river, with
     a wind-dapple here and there,
With ranging hills on the banks, with many a line against the
     sky, and shadows,
And the city at hand with dwellings so dense, and stacks of
     chimneys,
And all the scenes of life and the workshops, and the
     workmen homeward returning.

12

Lo, body and soul – this land,
My own Manhattan with spires, and the sparkling and
     hurrying tides, and the ships,   90

The varied and ample land, the South and the North in the
    light, Ohio's shores and flashing Missouri,
And ever the far-spreading prairies cover'd with grass and
    corn.

Lo, the most excellent sun so calm and haughty,
The violet and purple morn with just-felt breezes,
The gentle soft-born measureless light,
The miracle spreading bathing all, the fulfill'd noon,
The coming eve delicious, the welcome night and the stars,
Over my cities shining all, enveloping man and land.

13

Sing on, sing on you gray-brown bird,
Sing from the swamps, the recesses, pour your chant from the
    bushes,   100
Limitless out of the dusk, out of the cedars and pines.

Sing on dearest brother, warble your reedy song,
Loud human song, with voice of uttermost woe.

O liquid and free and tender!
O wild and loose to my soul – O wondrous singer!
You only I hear – yet the star holds me, (but will soon depart,)
Yet the lilac with mastering odor holds me.

14

Now while I sat in the day and look'd forth,
In the close of the day with its light and the fields of spring,
    and the farmers preparing their crops,
In the large unconscious scenery of my land with its lakes
    and forests,   110
In the heavenly aerial beauty, (after the perturb'd winds and
    the storms,)
Under the arching heavens of the afternoon swift passing,
    and the voices of children and women,
The many-moving sea-tides, and I saw the ships how they
    sail'd,
And the summer approaching with richness, and the fields
    all busy with labor,

And the infinite separate houses, how they all went on, each
    with its meals and minutia of daily usages,
And the streets how their throbbings throbb'd, and the cities
    pent – lo, then and there,
Falling upon them all and among them all, enveloping me
    with the rest,
Appear'd the cloud, appear'd the long black trail,
And I knew death, its thought, and the sacred knowledge of
    death.

Then with the knowledge of death as walking one side of me,   120
And the thought of death close-walking the other side of me,
And I in the middle as with companions, and as holding the
    hands of companions,
I fled forth to the hiding receiving night that talks not,
Down to the shores of the water, the path by the swamp in
    the dimness,
To the solemn shadowy cedars and ghostly pines so still.

And the singer so shy to the rest receiv'd me,
The gray-brown bird I know receiv'd us comrades three,
And he sang the carol of death, and a verse for him I love.

From deep secluded recesses,
From the fragrant cedars and the ghostly pines so still,   130
Came the carol of the bird.

And the charm of the carol rapt me,
As I held as if by their hands my comrades in the night,
And the voice of my spirit tallied the song of the bird.

Come lovely and soothing death,
Undulate round the world, serenely arriving, arriving,
In the day, in the night, to all, to each,
Sooner or later delicate death.

Prais'd be the fathomless universe,
For life and joy, and for objects and knowledge curious,   140
And for love, sweet love – but praise! praise! praise!
For the sure-enwinding arms of cool-enfolding death.

Dark mother always gliding near with soft feet,
Have none chanted for thee a chant of fullest welcome?
Then I chant it for thee, I glorify thee above all,
I bring thee a song that when thou must indeed come, come
    unfalteringly.

Approach strong deliveress,
When it is so, when thou hast taken them I joyously sing the dead,
Lost in the loving floating ocean of thee,
Laved in the flood of thy bliss O death.   150

From me to thee glad serenades,
Dances for thee I propose saluting thee, adornments and feastings
    for thee,
And the sights of the open landscape and the high-spread sky are
    fitting,
And life and the fields, and the huge and thoughtful night.

The night in silence under many a star,
The ocean shore and the husky whispering wave whose voice I
    know,
And the soul turning to thee O vast and well-veil'd death,
And the body gratefully nestling close to thee.

Over the tree-tops I float thee a song,
Over the rising and sinking waves, over the myriad fields and the
    prairies wide,   160
Over the dense-pack'd cities all and the teeming wharves and ways,
I float this carol with joy, with joy to thee O death.

15

To the tally of my soul,
Loud and strong kept up the gray-brown bird,
With pure deliberate notes spreading filling the night.

Loud in the pines and cedars dim,
Clear in the freshness moist and the swamp-perfume,
And I with my comrades there in the night.

While my sight that was bound in my eyes unclosed,

As to long panoramas of visions.   170

And I saw askant the armies,
I saw as in noiseless dreams hundreds of battle-flags,
Borne through the smoke of the battles and pierc'd with
    missiles I saw them,
And carried hither and yon through the smoke, and torn and
    bloody,
And at last but a few shreds left on the staffs, (and all in
    silence,)
And the staffs all splinter'd and broken.

I saw battle-corpses, myriads of them,
And the white skeletons of young men, I saw them,
I saw the debris and debris of all the slain soldiers of the war,
But I saw they were not as was thought,   180
They themselves were fully at rest, they suffer'd not,
The living remain'd and suffer'd, the mother suffer'd,
And the wife and the child and the musing comrade suffer'd,
And the armies that remain'd suffer'd.

                                16
Passing the visions, passing the night,
Passing, unloosing the hold of my comrades' hands,
Passing the song of the hermit bird and the tallying song of
    my soul,
Victorious song, death's outlet song, yet varying ever-
    altering song,
As low and wailing, yet clear the notes, rising and falling,
    flooding the night,
Sadly sinking and fainting, as warning and warning, and yet
    again bursting with joy,   190
Covering the earth and filling the spread of the heaven,
As that powerful psalm in the night I heard from recesses,
Passing, I leave thee lilac with heart-shaped leaves,
I leave thee there in the door-yard, blooming, returning with
    spring.

*

I cease from my song for thee,
From my gaze on thee in the west, fronting the west,
    communing with thee,
O comrade lustrous with silver face in the night.

Yet each to keep and all, retrievements out of the night,
The song, the wondrous chant of the gray-brown bird,
And the tallying chant, the echo arous'd in my soul,   200
With the lustrous and drooping star with the countenance
    full of woe,
With the holders holding my hand nearing the call of the bird,
Comrades mine and I in the midst, and their memory ever to
    keep, for the dead I loved so well,
For the sweetest, wisest soul of all my days and lands – and
    this for his dear sake,
Lilac and star and bird twined with the chant of my soul,
There in the fragrant pines and the cedars dusk and dim.

    1865–6   1881

When I Heard the Learn'd Astronomer

When I heard the learn'd astronomer,
When the proofs, the figures, were ranged in columns before
    me,
When I was shown the charts and diagrams, to add, divide,
    and measure them,
When I sitting heard the astronomer where he lectured with
    much applause in the lecture-room,
How soon unaccountable I became tired and sick,
Till rising and gliding out I wander'd off by myself,
In the mystical moist night-air, and from time to time,
Look'd up in perfect silence at the stars.

    1865   1865

A Noiseless Patient Spider

A noiseless patient spider,
I mark'd where on a little promontory it stood isolated,
Mark'd how to explore the vacant vast surrounding,
It launched forth, filament, filament, filament, out of itself,
Ever unreeling them, ever tirelessly speeding them.

And you O my soul where you stand,
Surrounded, detached, in measureless oceans of space,
Ceaselessly musing, venturing, throwing, seeking the spheres
    to connect them,
Till the bridge you will need be form'd, till the ductile anchor
    hold,
Till the gossamer thread you fling catch somewhere, O my
    soul.   10

1868   1881

Sparkles from the Wheel

Where the city's ceaseless crowd moves on the livelong day,
Withdrawn I join a group of children watching, I pause aside
    with them.

By the curb toward the edge of the flagging,
A knife-grinder works at his wheel sharpening a great knife,
Bending over he carefully holds it to the stone, by foot and
    knee,
With measur'd tread he turns rapidly, as he presses with light
    but firm hand,
Forth issue then in copious golden jets,
Sparkles from the wheel.

*

The scene and all its belongings, how they seize and affect me,
The sad sharp-chinn'd old man with worn clothes and broad
    shoulder-band of leather,   10
Myself effusing and fluid, a phantom curiously floating, now
    here absorb'd and arrested,
The group, (an unminded point set in a vast surrounding,)
The attentive, quiet children, the loud, proud, restive base of
    the streets,
The low hoarse purr of the whirling stone, the light-press'd
    blade,
Diffusing, dropping, sideways-darting, in tiny showers of
    gold,
Sparkles from the wheel.

    1871   1871

The Dalliance of the Eagles

Skirting the river road, (my forenoon walk, my rest,)
Skyward in air a sudden muffled sound, the dalliance of the
    eagles,
The rushing amorous contact high in space together,
The clinching interlocking claws, a living, fierce, gyrating
    wheel,
Four beating wings, two beaks, a swirling mass tight grap-
    pling,
In tumbling turning clustering loops, straight downward
    falling,
Till o'er the river pois'd, the twain yet one, a moment's lull,
A motionless still balance in the air, then parting, talons
    loosing,
Upward again on slow-firm pinions slanting, their separate
    diverse flight,
She hers, he his, pursuing.   10

    1880   1881

A Clear Midnight

This is thy hour O Soul, thy free flight into the wordless,
Away from books, away from art, the day erased, the lesson
    done,
Thee fully forth emerging, silent, gazing, pondering the
    themes thou lovest best,
Night, sleep, death and the stars.

  1881   1881

Notes

There was a Child Went Forth ll. 7–11 **Third-month . . . Fourth-month and Fifth-month:** Whitman liked to use Quaker terms for the months; these are March, April and May respectively. l. 34 **aureola:** radiant circle of light, as in a halo or an eclipse.

From: *Song of Myself* l. 95 **kelson:** keel; or timber used to fasten a ship's keel and floor together. l. 275 **jour printer:** journeyman printer: one who has served his apprenticeship and now works for a master. l. 279 **quadroon:** one-quarter negro by descent. l. 315 **Seventh-month:** Quaker term for July. l. 408 **carlacue:** a curlicue, a flourished inscription. l. 505 **afflatus:** inspiration. l. 530 **colter:** blade fixed to a ploughshare to part the soil. l. 613 **quahaug:** clam. l. 134 **Seventh-month:** Quaker term for July. l. 1290 **accoucheur:** French: a male midwife.

A Song for Occupations l. 56 **bon-mot:** French: a witty saying; **reconnoissance:** reconnaissance. l. 62 **camerado:** Spanish: comrade. l. 67 **savans:** French 'savants': learned people. l. 85 **Twelfth-month:** Quaker term for December. l. 109 **loup-lump:** the iron which gathers at the base of a blast furnace after iron oxide has been burned with coke and limestone. l. 116 **gutta-percha:** a plastic material made from the gum of trees. l. 120 **Stave-machines:** staves are thin strips of wood used to make up the sides of barrels.

The Sleepers l. 34 **douceurs:** French: pleasures. l. 35 **Cache:** French: hide.

Crossing Brooklyn Ferry l. 28 **Twelfth-month:** Quaker term for December.

Out of the Cradle Endlessly Rocking l. 3 **Ninth-month:** Quaker term for September. l. 23 **Paumanok:** Native American name for Long Island. l. 24 **Fifth-month:** Quaker term for May.

As I Ebb'd with the Ocean of Life l. 10 **windrows:** swathes of cut grass or other crops: hence, by extension, lines of sea-wrack carried by the tide and deposited on the beach.

In Paths Untrodden l. 15 **Ninth-month:** Quaker term for September.

Help us make the next generation of readers

We – both author and publisher – hope you enjoyed this book. We believe that you can become a reader at any time in your life, but we'd love your help to give the next generation a head start.

Did you know that 9 per cent of children don't have a book of their own in their home, rising to 13 per cent in disadvantaged families*? We'd like to try to change that by asking you to consider the role you could play in helping to build readers of the future.

We'd love you to think of sharing, borrowing, reading, buying or talking about a book with a child in your life and spreading the love of reading. We want to make sure the next generation continue to have access to books, wherever they come from.

And if you would like to consider donating to charities that help fund literacy projects, find out more at **www.literacytrust.org.uk** and **www.booktrust.org.uk**.

THANK YOU

*As reported by the National Literacy Trust